Stitch on the Double

Stitch *on the* Double

**Easy Quilt Projects
to Sew on the Go**

Kathleen Brown

Stitch on the Double:
Easy Quilt Projects to Sew on the Go
© 2015 by Kathleen Brown

Martingale®
19021 120th Ave. NE, Ste. 102
Bothell, WA 98011-9511 USA
ShopMartingale.com

Printed in China
20 19 18 17 16 15   8 7 6 5 4 3 2 1

Library of Congress Cataloging-in-Publication Data is available upon request.

ISBN: 978-1-60468-603-6

Mission Statement

Dedicated to providing quality products and service to inspire creativity.

Credits

PUBLISHER AND CHIEF VISIONARY OFFICER
Jennifer Erbe Keltner

EDITORIAL DIRECTOR
Karen Costello Soltys

DESIGN DIRECTOR
Paula Schlosser

ACQUISITIONS EDITOR
Karen M. Burns

PHOTOGRAPHER
Brent Kane

TECHNICAL EDITOR
Rebecca Kemp Brent

PRODUCTION MANAGER
Regina Girard

COPY EDITOR
Tiffany Mottet

COVER AND INTERIOR DESIGNER
Connor Chin

ILLUSTRATOR
Missy Shepler

Contents

Introduction

It's safe to say I love all things quilting: the fabrics, colors, felts, threads, and quilting methods. This industry has endless possibilities and everything tickles and encourages my senses. Making a quilt or table runner with colors and fabrics I'm normally drawn to is fun and rewarding, but then I love to take that same pattern, change the color placement, add some appliqué or embroidery, and enjoy it all over again.

I'm never without my sewing and find stitching by hand using Double Stitch a relaxing way to pass any spare time I have. The simple method of piecing by hand may sound scary, but rest assured, this is a simple running stitch with an appeal you'll love. Our lives are busy, but I've learned I can sew just about anywhere, and the conversations that start when someone sees me and asks about my stitching are always fun and interesting.

I call my piecing technique Double Stitch because it combines two lines of hand stitching along a single seam. The first line of running stitches actually creates the seam. It's followed by a second line of running stitches on the right side of the fabric, visible in the finished project.

Together, the running-stitch seam and the topstitching make Double Stitch. The effect is charming and relaxed rather than fine and exacting, so the technique is easy to master.

The projects I've included in this book range from framed art and wall hangings to table toppers, runners, and quilts, both lap-sized and larger. The ease of sewing with Double Stitch will make these take-along projects fun to complete. You'll be amazed at how much stitching you can do in as little as 15 minutes while waiting for an appointment or even on your lunch break at work. My favorite time to stitch, besides when I'm sitting next to a mountain stream, is when I'm sitting with my husband, watching a ball game on TV. He thinks we're having quality time together—which we are—but I get to stitch away on one of my projects. Blissful!

I believe you will find something unique here to sew for your home or make as a gift for someone special. Most of the projects are on a smaller scale, making them quick and easy to complete. It's my hope that after reading this book and trying a project or two, you'll fall in love with Double Stitch as I have.

Enjoy, and happy stitching!

The Double-Stitch Process

Most of us are familiar with sewing together pieces of fabric by machine, but I want to introduce you to a wonderfully charming method of hand piecing I call Double Stitch. The stitches are meant to be warm and primitive rather than tiny and precise, as with some other types of hand piecing. I call this no-stress sewing and piecing, and I mean it! The only stitch you need to master is a simple running stitch.

Double Stitch is worked in two steps as the name implies. First, you'll work a line of running stitches to sew a pair of patches together. Next, you'll stitch again from the right side of the fabric, creating a line of sewn-by-hand topstitching. The topstitching becomes an accent on your project that looks like hand quilting.

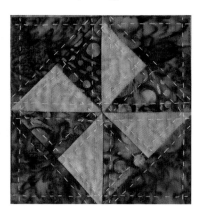

What You'll Need

Double Stitch is a take-along sewing method, so the supplies are simple. You may find that you already have most in your sewing stash.

Needles. Both Sharps and straw needles for hand sewing work well. Straw needles are a bit flexible and longer than Sharps, so you'll be able to comfortably sew several stitches at a time with them. Sharps have larger eyes, which makes them easier to thread. I prefer a size 11 needle with a big eye, but the type of needle you use is a personal choice. Try different sizes and lengths until you find one that you feel comfortable using.

Thread. Choose a 50-weight, 100% cotton sewing thread. I always use a neutral ecru color so that my stitching shows and is a highlight of the piece.

If you use thread that matches the fabric, your stitches will be less visible in the final piece. There's no need to use a coated quilting thread. It's more expensive and the coating isn't necessary.

Measuring tool. I prefer the aluminum measuring gauge from Nifty Notions for measuring seam allowances, as its size and durability make it perfect to keep in my sewing kit. However, you could also use a small ruler.

Goat's milk soap. Use the soap to condition the thread, reducing its tendency to twist and knot as you sew. After threading the needle, run the thread lightly over the soap once or twice—that's all there is to it! You'll need just a small chunk of the bar of soap, so share the rest with friends. You can substitute thread conditioner or a cake of beeswax if you prefer.

Other supplies. In addition, you'll need scissors and a thimble. That's it!

Doing Double Stitch

1 Thread the needle with a single strand of thread, drag the thread over the goat's milk soap to condition it, and knot the end of the thread.

2 Place two pieces of fabric right sides together, aligning the raw edges.

3 Measure and mark the seamline ¼" from the fabric edge on the wrong side of one piece. With experience, you may become comfortable judging the ¼" seam allowance by eye, without measuring. If you do mark, remember that these marks won't show on the final project. You can also slide the gauge along as you sew, measuring after you take several stitches.

4 Sew a running stitch along the line to join the pieces.

5 When you reach the end of the seam, take a small backstitch to secure the stitches, but *do not* cut the thread. The backstitch also reduces the possibility that you'll pull the stitches too hard, creating gathers or puckers, as you continue working.

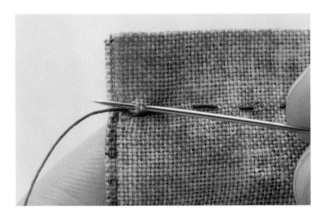

6 Open the fabric pieces and finger-press the seam allowances to one side. The project instructions will specify the correct pressing direction for all seam allowances.

Make a Sewing Kit

Gather all the items you'll need for hand piecing and keep them in a small sewing kit so you can take your sewing wherever you go. The container can be just about anything; you'll never look at a small tin, pencil box, cosmetic bag, decorative box, or even a zippered plastic bag the same way again! Be sure to include the following:

- 100% cotton ecru thread
- Hand-sewing needles
- Embroidery needles
- Embroidery scissors or a cutting pendant
- Thimble
- Measuring gauge or small ruler
- Goat's milk soap, beeswax, or thread conditioner
- Pearl cotton, size 8 or 12, or 6-strand embroidery floss (Because green and black are the colors needed for most of my embroidery, I always carry those colors with me. If a pattern calls for additional colors, I toss those in as well.)
- One or two small pieces of felted wool for holding needles and pins (Felt is flat, filling much less space than a pincushion.)

7 Flip the work over so that the right side is facing upward. Bring the threaded needle up through the seam allowances (fig. A) and sew a running stitch a scant ¼" from the seam (fig. B), catching the seam allowances and the top fabric with the stitches (fig. C). The topstitching holds the seam allowances in place and allows everything to lie nice and flat, without using an iron, for take-along flexibility.

Fig. A

Fig. B

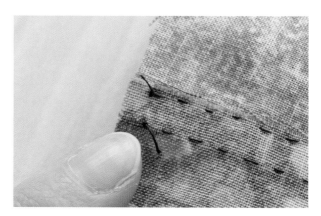

8 At the end of the seam, take the needle to the wrong side of the fabric, make a knot, and cut the thread.

Goat's Milk Soap

I'm sensitive to scents and aromas, so I use unscented goat's milk soap in my sewing kit as a thread conditioner. When shopping for a bar of goat's milk soap, look locally—you may be surprised at how readily available it is. A full-sized bar of soap will be too big for a small sewing kit and even a small chunk will last a very long time. Each bar of soap can easily yield six to eight chunks, so you can share with others who find themselves intrigued by Double Stitch.

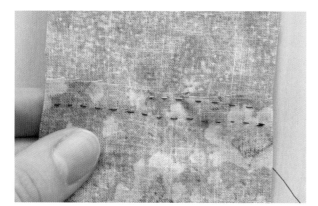

Fig. C

Matching Seams

Double-Stitch seams are a breeze to match. The seam allowances, pressed in opposite directions and topstitched, nest together to help secure the seam intersection as you stitch.

1 Place the pieced units to be joined with right sides together. Slide the layers between your fingers until you feel the seam allowances bump against each other. Pin the units together on both sides of the matching seams.

2 Using Double Stitch, sew the units together, finger-pressing the seam allowances as indicated in the project instructions.

Threaded Needles

To save time, especially if you hate threading needles, thread several needles at once and get that task out of the way!

Pull about 16" of thread from the spool, but *don't* cut it. Use a needle threader to place a dozen or so needles onto the thread. Wrap the needles and thread around the spool until needed. When the time comes, unwrap the thread, grab the first needle, and push the remaining needles farther down the string of thread until you have the necessary length of thread in the lone needle. Cut the thread, leaving the remaining needles threaded on the spool.

I love this little trick, especially when I'm sewing in the car. Have you ever tried to thread a needle while riding in an automobile?

Quilting a Double-Stitch Project

Quilting your project after it has been pieced is fun and easy. Depending on the type of project you're making, you can use batting or fusible fleece; the individual project instructions will guide you.

Fusible fleece should be applied after piecing, but before embroidery and embellishment, so that the iron's heat doesn't melt attached buttons or flatten the embroidery stitches. In contrast, non-fusible batting can be applied after embroidery and embellishment, which means you'll be embroidering through just the quilt top and not the thickness of the batting. Having a layer of fleece in place before embroidery makes it easier to hide thread ends while embroidering and adding buttons, so it may be the more appealing choice for beginning stitchers.

1 Following the manufacturer's instructions, apply fusible fleece or layer batting on the wrong side of the pieced project. Add embroidery or embellishments as directed in the project instructions and secure a layer of backing fabric over the fleece or batting if directed. Pin or baste the layers together.

2 You can see that most seams have a line of running stitches to one side, the second part of Double Stitch. To quilt the project, sew a new line of running stitches a scant ¼" from the unstitched side of each seam. Stitch through all the layers; however, the seam allowances will already be folded out of the way, so the thickness is lessened—another advantage of Double Stitch!

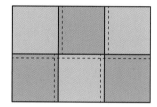

Double-Stitched seams

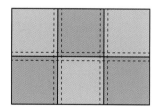

Quilt opposite sides of seamlines.

3 When the quilting is complete, frame or bind the project to finish it.

Hand Embroidery

Many of the projects are decorated with a bit of hand embroidery. I use just a few embroidery stitches. In case you're not familiar with them, each is illustrated below.

Backstitch

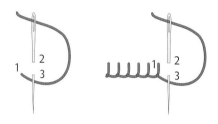

Blanket stitch

Lazy daisy stitch

Running stitch

To transfer the embroidery designs to a project, follow these steps:

1 Trace the pattern from the book onto a piece of plain paper. You may find it helpful to darken the tracing by going over the lines a second time with a black permanent marker.

2 Place the project over the tracing and trace the design onto the fabric with a water-soluble marker. A light box or sunny window makes this easier.

3 Embroider on the lines as directed in the project instructions. When the embroidery is complete, dab the project with a wet cloth to remove any markings that are still visible.

Button Details

I also enjoy adding buttons as a decorative detail. Look for small buttons, less than ¼" in diameter, in a variety of interesting shapes, as well as larger buttons that are ½" to ⅝" in diameter. If you collect buttons in various sizes and colors, you'll have a nice stash to pull from when choosing buttons for a specific project.

Framing

Of course, you can hire a professional to frame your finished Double-Stitch art, but you may want to try framing yourself. To frame any of the art pieces in this book, you'll need the following:

- Permanent spray adhesive
- Framing hardware: glazier's points, picture hanger, putty knife, and small hammer
- Foam board, cut to project measurements
- Frame with inside dimensions (from reveal to reveal) the same as the project

1 Spray one side of the foam board with adhesive and place it on a hard, flat surface with the adhesive side up. Be sure to protect surrounding surfaces from the overspray, and work in a well-ventilated area.

2 Spray the wrong side of the project with adhesive and carefully place the project on the foam board, matching the centers. Align the pieces well before placing them together as they will not be repositionable. Press down firmly, working from the center outward to the edges.

3 Place the mounted project in the frame. Insert the glazier's points into the frame, using a putty knife and small hammer if needed. These points hold the project in the frame.

4 Attach a picture hanger on the back of the frame at the center of the upper edge.

5 Optional: For a more finished look that also keeps out dust, cut a piece of heavy brown paper ½" to 1" larger than the opening in the back of the frame. Adhere the paper to the frame with heavy-duty double-sided tape, sealing the covered foam board in place.

Harvest Duo

Harvest time is always bursting with special, warm colors that hold appeal for several months. Nothing says harvest time better than a big, fat pumpkin and the many traditions surrounding this fun winter squash.

Harvest Art Piece

You'll be pleased with how quickly this framed art piece comes together.

Finished size: 14" x 14"

Materials

Yardage is based on 42"-wide fabric unless otherwise noted.

¼ yard of tan print for border

⅛ yard of beige print for background

⅛ yard of orange print for pumpkin

Scrap of brown felted wool for stem

Scrap of green felted wool for leaf

16" x 16" piece of fusible fleece

Pearl cotton or embroidery floss in brown, green, and black

9 buttons, ⅛" to ³⁄₁₆" diameter

Cutting

From the beige print, cut:
1 strip, 3½" x 42"; crosscut into 4 squares, 3½" x 3½"

From the orange print, cut:
1 strip, 3½" x 42"; crosscut into 9 squares, 3½" x 3½"

From the tan print, cut:
2 strips, 2¾" x 42"

Assembling the Block

1 Draw a diagonal line from corner to corner on the wrong side of each beige square.

2 Place a beige square on an orange square with right sides together. Sew a running stitch across the square on the drawn line. At the end of the seam, take a small backstitch, but *do not* cut the thread.

3 Trim the excess fabric, leaving ¼" seam allowances. Open the fabric pieces and finger-press the seam allowances toward the orange triangle.

4 Bring the threaded needle up through the seam allowances and sew a running stitch a scant ¼" from the seamline, catching both seam allowances, to topstitch the seam and complete the Double-Stitch join. When you reach the end of the seam, knot the thread on the wrong side and cut it. Make four half-square-triangle units.

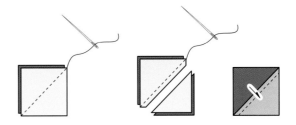

5 Arrange the half-square-triangle units and the remaining orange squares to form a pumpkin as shown in the photo on page 14.

6 Place the first two units in the top row with right sides together and join them, using Double Stitch (page 8). Finger-press the seam allowances toward the orange square and topstitch the seam.

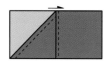

7 Using Double Stitch, add the third unit to the top row, finger-pressing the seam allowances toward the middle square.

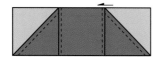

8 Assemble the other two rows of the block. For the middle row, finger-press the seam allowances toward the outside squares. For the bottom row, finger-press the seam allowances toward the middle square.

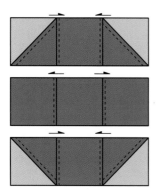

9 Join the rows, using Double Stitch. Nestle and match the intersecting seams, and pin the pieces before sewing if you wish. Finger-press the seam allowances downward before topstitching each seam.

Adding Borders

1 Measure the block through the center from top to bottom. Cut two pieces from the tan strips to this measurement (approximately 9½" long).

2 Using Double Stitch, sew a border strip to each side of the block, finger-pressing the seam allowances toward the border.

3 Measure the width of the block and border through the center. Cut two pieces from the tan strips to this measurement (approximately 14" long).

4 Use Double Stitch to sew the border strips to the top and bottom edges of the assembled unit, finger-pressing the seam allowances toward the border.

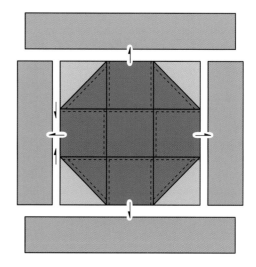

Finishing

1 Transfer the embroidery designs from page 12 onto the block, referring to "Hand Embroidery" on page 14 for instructions and the photo for placement.

2 Measure the block; cut a piece of fusible fleece the same size (approximately 14" square). Follow the manufacturer's instructions to fuse the fleece to the wrong side of the block.

3 Using the patterns on page 17, cut one stem from the brown wool and one leaf from the green wool. Pin the stem and leaf to the block, referring to the photo for placement. Blanket-stitch around each piece, using a single strand of pearl cotton or three strands of embroidery floss.

4 Referring to "Quilting a Double-Stitch Project" on page 11, sew a running stitch through all layers a scant ¼" from each seam on the side without topstitching. When the quilting is complete, each seam will have stitching on both sides.

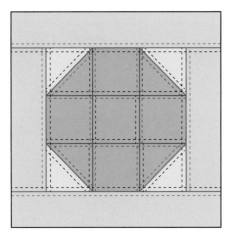

Quilting diagram

5 Embroider the tendrils with a backstitch, using a single strand of pearl cotton or three strands of embroidery floss. Embellish the quilt by stitching several small buttons along the tendrils, referring to the project photo for placement.

6 Follow the instructions in "Framing" on page 13 to frame the finished quilt.

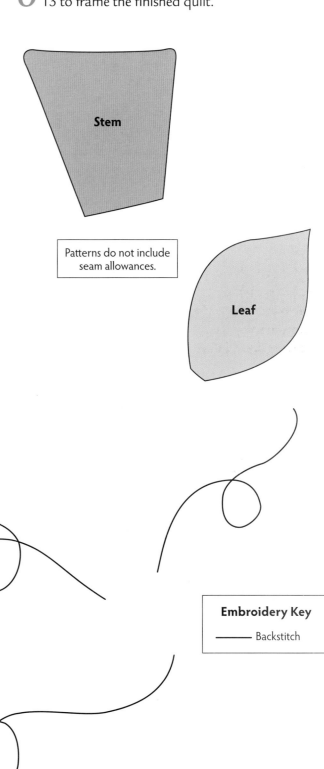

Stem

Patterns do not include
seam allowances.

Leaf

Embroidery Key
—— Backstitch

Harvest Table Topper

A seasonal table topper is a great way to coordinate room decor. Can't you picture so many of your current decorations centered on these pumpkins, cheering up the room?

Finished size: 29½" x 29½"

Materials

Yardage is based on 42"-wide fabric unless otherwise noted. Fat eighths measure approximately 9" x 21".

1 fat eighth *each* of 4 different orange prints for pumpkins

⅜ yard of tan print #4 for outer border

¼ yard of tan print #1 for background

¼ yard *each* of tan prints #2 and #3 for inner borders

3" x 9" piece of brown felted wool for stems

2" x 8" piece of green felted wool for leaves

⅜ yard of dark-brown print for binding

1 yard of fabric for backing

32" x 32" piece of batting

Pearl cotton or embroidery floss in black, brown, and green

36 buttons, ⅛" to 3⁄16" diameter

Cutting

From tan print #1, cut:
2 strips, 3½" x 42"; crosscut into 16 squares, 3½" x 3½"

From *each* of the orange-print fat eighths, cut:
9 squares, 3½" x 3½" (36 total)

From tan print #2, cut:
3 strips, 2" x 42"

From tan print #3, cut:
3 strips, 2" x 42"

From tan print #4, cut:
4 strips, 3" x 42"

From the dark-brown print, cut:
4 strips, 2¼" x 42"

Assembling the Blocks

1. Draw a diagonal line from corner to corner on the wrong side of each tan #1 square.

2. Place a marked square on an orange square with right sides together. Sew a running stitch across the square on the drawn line. When you reach the end of the seam, take a small backstitch, but *do not* cut the thread.

3. Trim the excess fabric, leaving ¼" seam allowances. Open the fabric pieces and finger-press the seam allowances toward the orange triangle.

4. Bring the needle up through the seam allowances and sew a running stitch a scant ¼" from the seam, catching the seam allowances in the topstitching. When you reach the end of the seam, knot the thread on the wrong side and cut it. Make four half-square-triangle units with *each* of the four orange prints, for a total of 16.

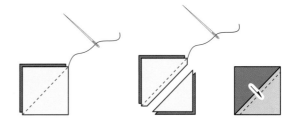

5. Arrange the half-square-triangle units and the remaining orange squares of a single print to form a pumpkin. Join the first two units in the top row, using Double Stitch (page 8). Finger-press the seam allowances toward the orange square.

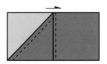

6. Add the third square in the top row, using Double Stitch. Finger-press the seam allowances toward the middle square.

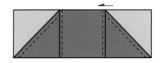

7 Assemble the middle and bottom rows, using Double Stitch. Finger-press the seam allowances toward the outside squares in the middle row, and toward the middle square in the bottom row.

8 Join the rows, using Double Stitch. Nestle the seam allowances and match the seams. Pin before sewing if you wish. Finger-press the seam allowances downward. Make four pumpkin blocks, one from each orange print.

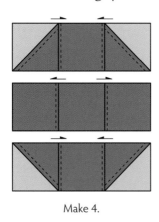

Make 4.

Assembling the Quilt Top

1 Use tan print #2 for the inner border around the first pumpkin block. Measure the block through the center from top to bottom. Cut two pieces from the tan 2" x 42" strips to this measurement (approximately 9½" long).

2 Using Double Stitch, sew a border strip to each side of the block, finger-pressing the seam allowances toward the border.

3 Measure the width of the block and border through the center. Cut two pieces from the tan 2" x 42" strips to this measurement (approximately 12½" long).

4 Attach the top and bottom border strips, using Double Stitch. Finger-press the seam allowances toward the border.

5 Repeat steps 1–4 to make four bordered pumpkin blocks—two with tan print #2 and two with tan print #3. Arrange the four blocks as shown in the quilt assembly diagram above right. If you used directional fabrics, be sure to orient the prints as shown in the photo on page 18.

6 Sew each row of two pumpkin blocks together, using Double Stitch. Finger-press the seam allowances as shown.

7 Using Double Stitch, join the rows, matching the seams at the center. Finger-press the seam allowances downward.

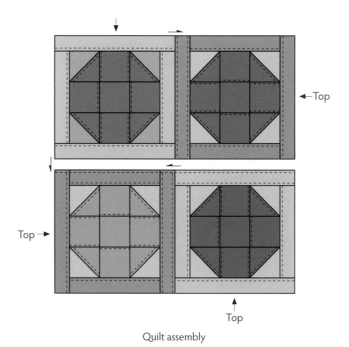

Quilt assembly

Adding Borders

1 Measure the quilt top through the center from top to bottom. Cut two pieces from the tan #4 strips to that measurement (approximately 24½" long).

2 Sew a border strip to each side of the quilt top, using Double Stitch. Press the seam allowances toward the border.

3 Measure the width of the quilt top, including the side borders, through the center. Cut two pieces from the tan #4 strips to that measurement (approximately 29½" long).

4 Use Double Stitch to sew the border strips to the top and bottom edges of the quilt. Press the seam allowances toward the border.

Finishing

1 Using the patterns on page 17, cut four stems from the brown wool and four leaves from the green wool. Pin the appliqués to the quilt, referring to the photo on page 18. Blanket-stitch around each piece, using a single strand of pearl cotton or three strands of embroidery floss.

2 Transfer the embroidery designs from page 17 onto the quilt, referring to "Hand Embroidery" on page 12 for instructions and the photo for placement. Embroider the tendrils with a backstitch, using a single strand of pearl cotton or three strands of embroidery floss. Stitch several small buttons along the tendrils.

3 Layer the backing, batting, and quilt top. Pin or baste the layers together.

4 Referring to "Quilting a Double-Stitch Project" on page 11, sew a running stitch through all layers a scant ¼" from each seam on the side

without topstitching. When the quilting is complete, each seam will have stitching on both sides.

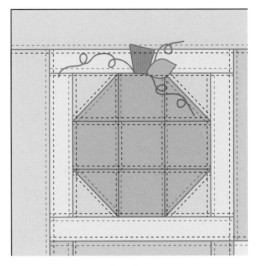

Quilting diagram

5 Trim the backing and batting even with the quilt top.

6 Join the dark-brown strips to make a continuous length and use it to bind the quilt. For free, downloadable binding instructions, go to ShopMartingale.com/HowtoQuilt.

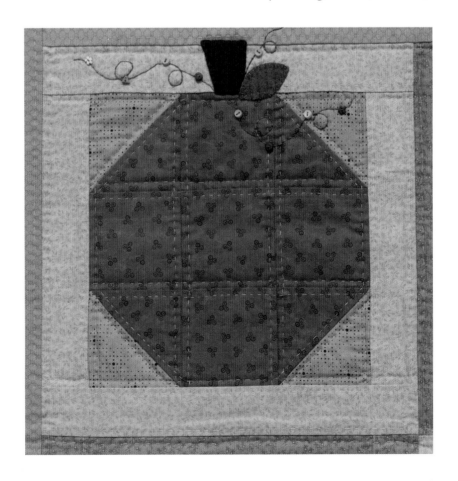

Gentle Breeze Duo

Bring a bit of the garden and its refreshing breeze inside to enjoy throughout the year with this bed quilt and throw-pillow combo.

Gentle Breeze Pillow

Double-Stitch patchwork creates a colorful background for a playful appliqué blossom.

Finished Size: 16" x 16"

Materials

Yardage is based on 42"-wide fabric unless otherwise noted.

½ yard of tan print for background and outer border

⅛ yard *each* of 4 different medium to dark batiks for pinwheels

⅛ yard of dark-brown batik for inner border

Scraps of batik fabrics for appliqué: red for coneflower, green for leaves and stem, and dark brown for cone

½ yard of dark-brown print for pillow back

18" x 18" piece of fusible fleece

16" x 16" pillow form

Lightweight fusible web

Pearl cotton or embroidery floss in red, brown, and green

Cutting

From the tan print, cut:

2 strips, 2½" x 42"; crosscut into 20 squares, 2½" x 2½"

1 strip, 4½" x 42"; crosscut into 4 squares, 4½" x 4½"

2 strips, 2" x 42"

From *each* of the medium to dark batiks, cut:

1 strip, 2½" x 42"; crosscut into 5 squares, 2½" x 2½" (20 total)

From the dark-brown batik, cut:

2 strips, 1" x 42"

From the dark-brown print, cut:*

1 rectangle, 16½" x 22"

1 rectangle, 16½" x 20"

*Before cutting, see "Finishing" on page 25.

Assembling the Pillow Front

1 Draw a diagonal line from corner to corner on the wrong side of each tan 2½" square.

2 Place a marked square on a medium- to dark-batik square with right sides together. Sew a running stitch along the drawn line. When you reach the end of the seam, take a small backstitch, but *do not* cut the thread.

3 Trim the excess fabric, leaving ¼" seam allowances. Open the fabric pieces and finger-press the seam allowances toward the batik triangle.

4 Bring the threaded needle to the right side of the fabric and sew a running stitch a scant ¼" from the seam, catching the seam allowances with the topstitching. At the end of the seam, knot the thread on the wrong side and cut it. Make 20 half-square-triangle units.

5 Arrange the half-square-triangle units to form five pinwheel units. Working on one pinwheel at a time, join the half-square-triangle units in pairs, using Double Stitch (page 8). Finger-press the seam allowances toward the batik triangles as shown.

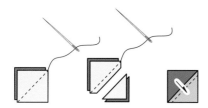

6 Sew two pairs together to make a pinwheel unit, matching the intersecting seams. Use Double Stitch, finger-pressing the seam allowances downward. Make five pinwheel units.

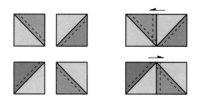

Make 5.

7 Arrange the tan 4½" squares and the pinwheel units as shown above right. Using Double Stitch, join the units in rows. Finger-press the seam allowances toward the tan squares. Join the rows using Double Stitch. Match the seam

intersections, and pin before sewing if you wish. Finger-press the seam allowances downward.

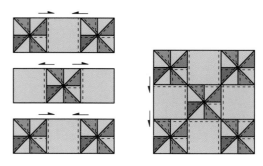

Adding Borders

1 Measure the block through the center from top to bottom. Cut two pieces from the dark-brown strips to this measurement (approximately 12½" long).

2 Using Double Stitch, sew a border strip to each side of the pieced block and press the seam allowances toward the border.

3 Measure the width of the block and border through the center. Cut two pieces from the dark-brown strips to this measurement (approximately 13½" long).

4 Use Double Stitch to sew the border strips to the top and bottom edges of the assembled unit, finger-pressing the seam allowances toward the border.

5 Repeat steps 1–4 to cut and attach the outer border. Use the tan 2"-wide strips, and cut the border pieces approximately 13½" and 16½" long.

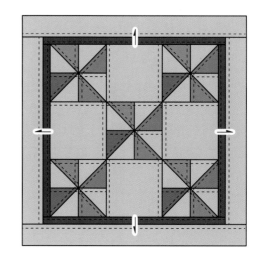

Appliquéing and Quilting

1 Using the patterns on page 26 and scraps of batik fabrics, prepare four petals, two leaves, and one cone for your favorite appliqué method. I used fusible appliqué and blanket-stitched the edges by hand.

2 For the stem, cut a rectangle of green fabric, 1¼" x 6½". Fold the strip in half lengthwise with *wrong* sides together and stitch the long raw edges using a ⅛" seam allowance. Flatten the fabric tube, centering the seam allowances on the wrong side and finger-pressing them to one side.

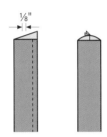

3 Referring to the photo on page 22, arrange the coneflower, stem, and leaves on the pillow front, tucking the ends under neighboring appliqué elements where appropriate, and pin in place. The stem's seam allowances will be hidden between the stem and background. Appliqué the pieces to the pillow front.

Appliqué Know-How

For free, downloadable information about appliqué techniques, visit ShopMartingale.com/HowtoQuilt.

---

4 Measure the pillow front and cut a piece of fusible fleece the same size (approximately 16½" x 16½"). Following the manufacturer's instructions, fuse the fleece to the wrong side of the pillow front.

5 To quilt, sew a running stitch through all the layers, placing the stitches a scant ¼" from the side of each seam that hasn't been topstitched. When the quilting is complete, every seam, including the borders, will have stitching on both sides.

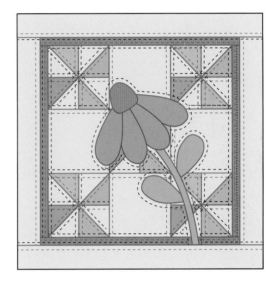

Quilting diagram

Finishing

I used simple overlapping flaps for the pillow back, but you can use another method if you prefer. Begin by measuring your pillow front, which should be approximately 16½" x 16½"; if not, adjust the 16½" measurements in step 1 to match your pillow front.

1 Fold the two dark-brown backing rectangles in half, wrong sides together, and press. Piece A will measure 16½" x 11" when folded, and piece B will be 16½" x 10".

2 Place piece A on the pillow front with right sides together, aligning the raw edges.

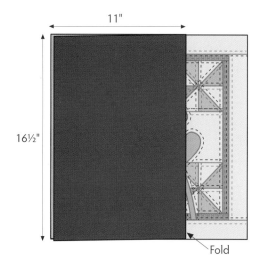

Fold

3 Lay piece B on top, aligning the raw edges on the opposite side of the pillow front. The folded edges of the pillow backs will overlap. Pin

the layers together along the raw edges, especially at the corners and overlapped areas.

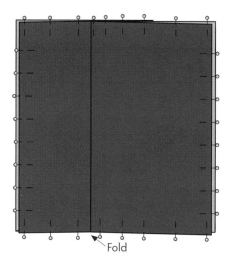

Fold

4 Using a ¼" seam allowance, sew around the entire pillow cover with your sewing machine.

5 Turn the pillow cover right side out through the opening in the pillow back. Gently smooth the corners into shape. Insert the pillow form through the opening in the back.

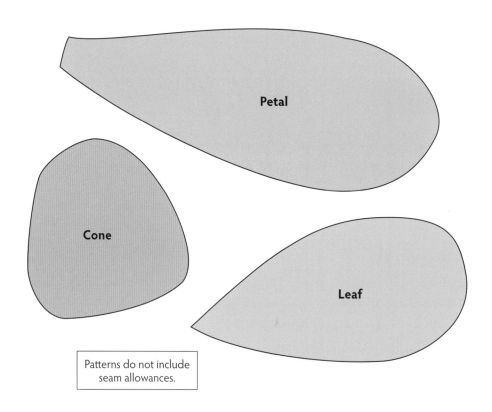

Petal

Cone

Leaf

Patterns do not include seam allowances.

Gentle Breeze Quilt

*You can almost see the movement of the pinwheels
and the coneflowers when a gentle breeze comes along.*

Finished size: 72" x 93"

Block size: 10½" x 10½"

Materials

Yardage is based on 42"-wide fabric unless otherwise noted. Fat quarters measure approximately 18" x 21".

3¾ yards of beige print for pinwheels and outer border

2 yards *total* of assorted tan prints for appliqué blocks (sample uses 11" squares of 17 different fabrics)

1¼ yards of black print for inner border and binding

1 yard *total* of assorted medium and dark prints for pinwheels

½ yard *total* of assorted prints for appliquéd flowers (sample uses 5" x 7" pieces of 17 different fabrics)

1 fat quarter of green floral for leaves

1 fat quarter of green print for stems

⅛ yard of dark-brown print for flower cones

5½ yards of fabric for backing

78" x 99" piece of batting

Freezer paper

Appliqué glue

Scrap Happy

For added interest, use some of your scraps for the appliquéd flowers, or even for the pinwheel blocks.

Cutting

From the beige print, cut:

12 strips, 2⅝" x 42"; crosscut into 180 squares, 2⅝" x 2⅝"

8 strips, 4" x 42"; crosscut into 72 squares, 4" x 4"

8 strips, 8" x 42"

From the assorted medium and dark prints, cut:

180 squares, 2⅝" x 2⅝"

From the green print, cut:

17 rectangles, 1¼" x 6½"

From the assorted tan prints, cut:

17 squares, 11" x 11"

From the black print, cut:

8 strips, 2½" x 42"

9 strips, 2¼" x 42"

Assembling the Blocks

Machine stitching will make this quilt easier and quicker to construct as well as more durable, but keep that wonderful hand stitching where it is visible on your quilt top.

1 Draw a diagonal line on the wrong side of each beige 2⅝" square.

2 Place a marked square on a medium or dark 2⅝" square with right sides together. Sew a running stitch ¼" from the drawn line on both sides. When you reach the end of a seam, knot the thread on the wrong side and cut it. This step can be sewn by machine.

3 Cut along the drawn line to create two units. Finger-press the seam allowances toward the darker triangles.

4 Sew a running stitch a scant ¼" from the seam. Be sure to catch the seam allowances with the topstitching. At the end of the seam, knot the thread on the wrong side and cut it. Make 360.

Make 360.

5 Arrange four half-square-triangle units in the same print to make a pinwheel unit. Join the units into pairs using Double Stitch (page 8).

6 Open each pair and finger-press the seam allowances toward the darker triangle as shown. Add topstitching to complete the Double-Stitch process.

7 Using Double Stitch, sew the two pairs together to make a pinwheel unit, matching the seams at the center and pressing the seam allowances downward. The seam allowances at the center will nestle together nicely; pin the layers before stitching if you wish. Make 90.

Make 90.

8 Arrange five pinwheel units and four beige 4" squares to make a pinwheel block.

9 Using Double Stitch, join the units in rows. Finger-press the seam allowances toward the beige squares in each row.

10 Using Double Stitch, join the rows, matching the intersecting seams. Finger-press the seam allowances downward. Make 18 pinwheel blocks.

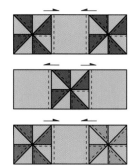
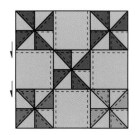

Make 18.

Appliquéing

1 Using the patterns on page 32, prepare four petals, one leaf, and one cone for *each* of the appliqué blocks. Choose a single fabric for all four petals on an individual block. Use your favorite appliqué method; for the sample, the shapes were traced onto freezer paper in preparation for needle-turn appliqué. The patterns do not include seam allowances, so remember to add them if needed for your chosen appliqué method.

2 For each stem, fold a green-print rectangle in half, lengthwise, with *wrong* sides together. Stitch the long raw edges, using a ⅛" seam allowance. Flatten the fabric tube, centering the seam allowances on the wrong side and finger-pressing them to one side.

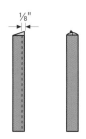

3 Using the photo on page 28 as a guide, arrange the petals, leaf, stem, and cone for one block on an 11" square and pin in place. Overlap the edges of the appliqué shapes where appropriate. The stem's seam allowances will be hidden between the stem and background. Stitch the appliqués to the background fabric. Make 17 coneflower blocks, varying the stem shapes and direction of the flower heads so the flowers appear to be blowing in a gentle breeze.

Assembling the Quilt Top

1 Arrange all the blocks as shown in the quilt assembly diagram on page 31, alternating pinwheel and coneflower blocks. Join the blocks in rows by hand or machine, but sew the topstitching by hand after pressing the seam allowances toward the coneflower blocks.

2 Join the rows by hand or machine, but again, the topstitching should be sewn by hand. Finger-press the seam allowances downward.

Adding Borders

1 Measure the quilt top through the center from top to bottom. Sew two 2½"-wide black strips together end to end and cut a border strip to match the quilt measurement (approximately 74" long). Make two.

2 Sew a border strip to each side of the quilt top by machine, but sew the topstitching by hand after pressing the seam allowances toward the border strip.

3 Measure the width of the quilt top, including the side borders, through the center. Sew two black 2½"-wide strips together end to end and trim to this measurement (approximately 57" long). Make two. Repeat step 2 to attach the border strips to the top and bottom edges of the quilt. Topstitch by hand.

4 Repeat steps 1–3, using the beige 8"-wide strips to add the outer border to the quilt top. The border pieces will measure approximately 78" and 72" long.

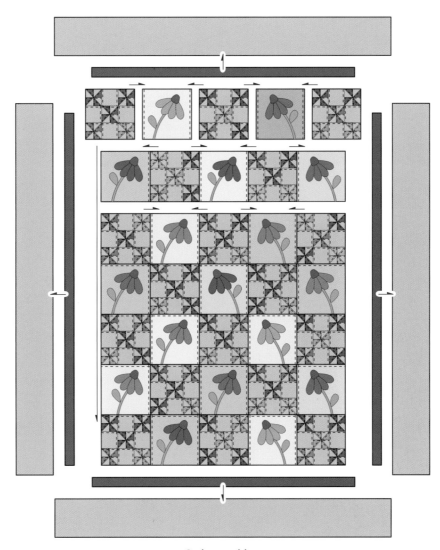

Quilt assembly

Finishing

1 Cut the backing fabric into two lengths of 99". Remove the selvages, sew the two pieces together along one long edge, and press the seam allowances open.

2 Layer the backing, batting, and quilt top. Pin or baste the layers together.

3 Referring to "Quilting a Double-Stitch Project" on page 11, sew a running stitch through all layers a scant ¼" from each seam on the side without topstitching. When the quilting is complete, each seam will have stitching on both sides. In addition, echo quilt the coneflower blocks with running stitches that repeat the appliqué shapes. Pick a quilting pattern for the borders and stitch through all the layers with the same simple running stitch.

4 Trim the backing and batting even with the quilt top.

5 Join the black 2¼"-wide strips to make a continuous length and use it to bind the quilt. For free, downloadable binding instructions, go to ShopMartingale.com/HowtoQuilt.

Quilting diagram

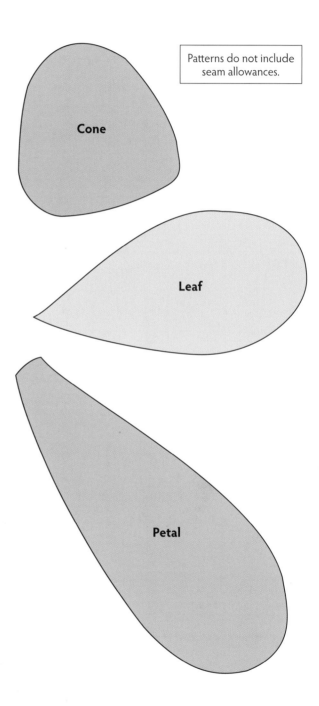

Patterns do not include seam allowances.

Cone

Leaf

Petal

Gift for You

Happy Birthday

This table runner sets the tone for a party and can
be a great addition to any decorations or theme you
plan. Surrounded by cake, candles, and plates or a pile
of unopened presents, this runner is just cute!

Designed by Kathleen Brown; made by Anne Styles
Finished size: 37½" x 21½"

Materials

*Yardage is based on 42"-wide fabric unless otherwise
noted. Fat eighths measure approximately 9" x 21".*

⅔ yard of tan print for background, sashing,
and inner and outer borders

½ yard of green print for middle border
and binding

¼ yard of red print for ribbons and bows

⅛ yard (or 1 fat eighth) *each* of 3 assorted fabrics
for packages

⅔ yard of fabric for backing

40" x 24" piece of fusible fleece

Pearl cotton or embroidery floss in green and
black

16 buttons, ⅛" to ³⁄₁₆" diameter

Fabric Fun

Imagine all the fun fabrics you could
"wrap" these packages in. Use your scraps
or a coordinated group of fabrics that
catches your eye. To personalize the project,
embroider a name and date as well as
"Happy Birthday," or switch the message to
suit any special occasion.

Cutting

From the red print, cut:
2 strips, 1½" x 42"; crosscut into:
6 rectangles, 1½" x 3½"
3 rectangles, 1½" x 7½"
1 strip, 2½" x 42"; crosscut into 6 squares,
2½" x 2½"

From *each* of the assorted fabrics, cut:
4 squares, 3½" x 3½" (12 total)

From the tan print, cut:
2 strips, 2½" x 42"; crosscut *1 of the strips*
(reserving the second strip for sashing) into:
9 rectangles, 1½" x 2½"
6 squares, 2½" x 2½"
3 strips, 3½" x 42"
2 strips, 2" x 42"

From the green print, cut:
3 strips, 2" x 42"
4 strips, 2¼" x 42"

Assembling the Table Runner

1 Arrange the fabric pieces for each package
block. Work on one block at a time.

2 Lay a red 1½" x 3½" rectangle on one
assorted-fabric square and join them with
Double Stitch (page 8). Finger-press the seam
allowances toward the square.

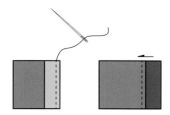

3 Use Double Stitch to sew a second assorted-fabric square on the other side of the red rectangle. Finger-press the seam allowances toward the new square. Make two package units.

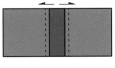

Make 2.

4 Lay a red 1½" x 7½" rectangle on one of the package units and join them with Double Stitch. Finger-press the seam allowances toward the red rectangle.

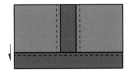

5 Using Double Stitch, sew the second package unit to the other long edge of the red rectangle. Finger-press the seam allowances toward the red rectangle.

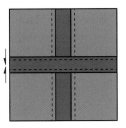

6 Repeat steps 1–5 to make two more package blocks.

7 Referring to the diagram in step 9 on page 36, draw a diagonal line from corner to corner on the wrong side of each tan 2½" square. Place a marked square on a red 2½" square with right sides together. Sew a running stitch on the drawn line. When you reach the end of the seam, take a backstitch, but *do not* cut the thread.

8 Trim the excess fabric, leaving ¼" seam allowances. Open the fabric pieces and finger-press the seam allowances toward the red triangle.

9 Sew a running stitch a scant ¼" from the seam on the red fabric to complete the Double-Stitch process, catching the seam allowances in the topstitching. When you reach the end of the seam, knot the thread on the wrong side and cut it. Make six half-square-triangle units.

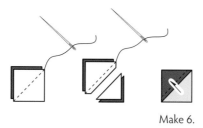

Make 6.

10 Using Double Stitch, sew a tan 1½" x 2½" rectangle to one side of a half-square-triangle unit as shown. Finger-press the seam allowances toward the rectangle. Using Double Stitch, sew a second half-square-triangle unit to the other side of the tan rectangle. Add a tan rectangle to each end of the unit. Notice that all of the seam allowances are pressed toward the tan rectangles. Make three bow units.

Make 3.

11 Lay a bow unit on a package block with right sides together, matching the center seams. Pin before sewing if you wish. Using Double Stitch, join the units, finger-pressing the seam allowances toward the package block. Make three.

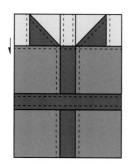

Make 3.

Adding Sashing and Borders

1 Measure the blocks through their centers from top to bottom and average the measurements. Cut two pieces of the remaining tan 2½"-wide strip to the average measurement (approximately 9½" long).

2 Arrange the three package blocks as desired with the sashing strips between the blocks. Use Double Stitch to join the units, finger-pressing the seam allowances toward the sashing strips.

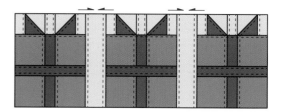

3 From each tan 2"-wide strip, cut one rectangle to the average measurement from step 1 for the side inner borders. Using Double Stitch, sew the rectangles to the ends of the assembled row, pressing the seam allowances toward the border strips.

4 Measure the width of the blocks and border strips through the center. Cut one piece from each tan 2"-wide strip to this measurement (approximately 28½" long). Using Double Stitch, sew these strips to the top and bottom edges of the assembled row. Press the seam allowances toward the border.

5 Measure, cut, and add the middle border in the same way, using the green 2"-wide strips. The border strips will be cut approximately 12½" and 31½" long. Press the seam allowances toward the green border.

6 Measure, cut, and add the outer border in the same way, using the tan 3½"-wide strips. The border strips will be cut approximately 15½" and 37½" long. Press the seam allowances toward the outer border.

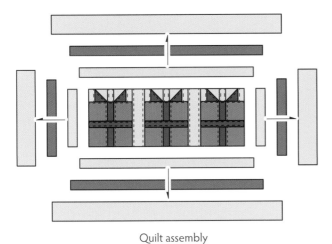

Quilt assembly

Finishing

1 Transfer the embroidery designs from page 38 onto the outer border of the table runner, referring to "Hand Embroidery" on page 12 for instructions and the photo on page 35 for placement. Reverse the design to fit on the border on the right-hand side.

2 Measure the table runner and cut a piece of fusible fleece the same size (approximately 37½" x 21½"). Following the manufacturer's instructions, fuse the fleece to the back of the table runner.

3 Embroider the designs with one strand of pearl cotton or three strands of embroidery floss, using green for the vines and leaves, and black for the letters. Use a backstitch for the vines and letters and a lazy daisy stitch for the leaves. Embellish with several small buttons along the vines, referring to the photo for placement.

4 To quilt the table runner, refer to "Quilting a Double-Stitch Project" on page 11. Center the runner on the wrong side of the backing fabric and pin or baste the layers. Quilt through all the layers, using the same running stitch used to piece the table runner, sewing a scant ¼" from each seam on the side without topstitching. When the quilting is complete, each seam will have stitching

on both sides. Feel free to add additional quilting on the runner's open areas as desired.

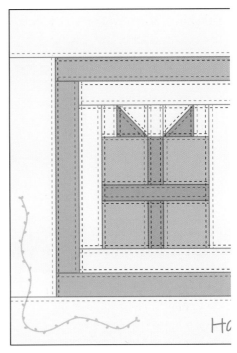

Quilting diagram

5 Trim the backing fabric even with the table-runner top.

6 Join the green 2¼"-wide strips to make a continuous length and use it to bind the runner. For free, downloadable binding instructions, go to ShopMartingale.com/HowtoQuilt.

Happy Birthday

Embroidery Key

—— Backstitch

⟐ Lazy daisy

Embroidery for left side; reverse for right side.

Who, Me?

*H*ere's a woodland creature for any decor, designed to make beautiful use of leftover fabric bits.

Materials

Yardage is based on 42"-wide fabric unless otherwise noted.

¼ yard of tan print for outer border

⅛ yard of dark-brown print for inner border

8½" x 8½" square of muslin

6" x 6" square of red print for owl

6 to 10 scrap strips (strings) of fabric in light green, yellow, brown, and tan for background

Scraps of assorted fabrics for wings, feet, eyes, and beak

16" x 16" piece of fusible fleece

Pearl cotton or embroidery floss in black and green

2 light-colored triangular buttons, about ¼" wide, for eyes

String Theory

This project uses what quilters call "strings"—the uneven ends of fabric that are typically trimmed off after the fabric has been washed and dried. As you square the end of prewashed fabric, cut off a couple of inches along the ratty edge, toss them into a basket, and watch your stash grow. Those strings are perfect for projects like this one.

Cutting

From the dark-brown print, cut:
1 strip, 1½" x 42"; crosscut into:
2 rectangles, 1½" x 8½"
2 rectangles, 1½" x 10½"

From the tan print, cut:
2 strips, 2¼" x 42"; crosscut into:
2 rectangles, 2¼" x 10½"
2 rectangles, 2¼" x 14"

Assembling the Block

1 Arrange the fabric strings for the background, using any prints and colors you wish. Position one medium- to dark-brown string just below the halfway point to create a branch for the owl to sit upon.

2 Lay the muslin foundation square on a flat surface and place a string along the top edge of the muslin, right side up. Don't try to align the top or side edges; just let the string hang over the top and sides of the muslin.

3 Place the second string on the first string, right sides together, aligning only the lower edges, which may be straight or at an angle.

4 Attach the strings to the foundation, using Double Stitch (page 8). Sew the first running stitches ¼" from the aligned edges of the strings, sewing through the strings and foundation. When you reach the end of the *foundation*, take a backstitch to secure the thread, but *do not* cut the thread.

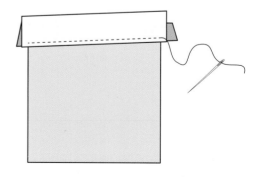

5 Finger-press the second fabric string downward on top of the foundation muslin. Bring the needle up through the foundation, seam allowances, and string fabric to sew a running stitch a scant ¼" from the seam. Be sure to catch the seam allowances in this topstitching. When you have stitched back to the beginning edge of the *foundation*, knot the thread on the wrong side and cut it. There is no need to trim the strings as you progress; just allow them to extend beyond the foundation's edges until you are finished adding strings.

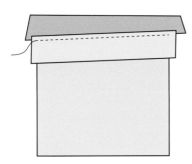

6 Lay a new string on the previous strings, right sides together, aligning its raw edge with the lower edge of the string just added. Attach the new string, using Double Stitch.

7 Continue adding strings until you have covered the entire muslin foundation. Remember to sew a brown strip onto the foundation to represent a branch for the owl. When the piecing is complete, trim the edges of the strings even with the muslin foundation, creating a pieced 8½" square.

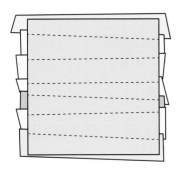
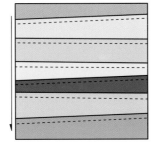

Adding Borders

1 Using Double Stitch, sew a dark-brown 1½" x 8½" rectangle to each side of the pieced unit. Finger-press the seam allowances toward the border.

2 Using Double Stitch, sew the dark-brown 1½" x 10½" rectangles to the top and bottom edges of the assembled unit. Finger-press the seam allowances toward the border.

3 Repeat steps 1 and 2 to attach the tan 2¼"-wide outer border. Finger-press the seam allowances toward the outer border.

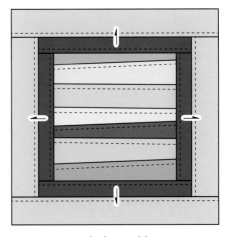

Block assembly

Appliquéing and Finishing

1 Measure the pieced block and cut a piece of fusible fleece the same size (approximately 14" x 14"). Follow the manufacturer's instructions to fuse the fleece to the wrong side of the block.

2 Use the patterns on page 42 to prepare the appliqués for your favorite method. Cut one each of the body and beak patterns, and two each of the foot, wing, eye, and inner-eye patterns. Position the prepared appliqués on the pieced block and stitch in place with your chosen method. For the sample, the appliqués were attached with fusible web and hand-embroidery stitches: blanket stitch for the body, wings, and eyes, and a running stitch around the beak and feet. Use one strand of pearl cotton or three strands of embroidery floss. Stitch a small triangle button to each eye as a highlight, referring to the photo on page 39 for placement.

Shape Up

If you don't have tiny triangular buttons, substitute round buttons of a similar size.

3 Referring to "Quilting a Double-Stitch Project" on page 11, sew a running stitch through all layers a scant ¼" from each seam on the side without topstitching. When the quilting is complete, each seam will have stitching on both sides. In addition, quilt a scant ¼" outside the appliquéd owl to further define the shape.

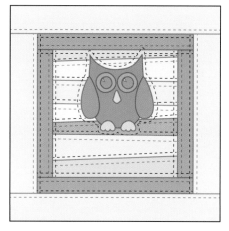

Quilting diagram

4 Follow the instructions in "Framing" on page 13 to frame the finished quilt.

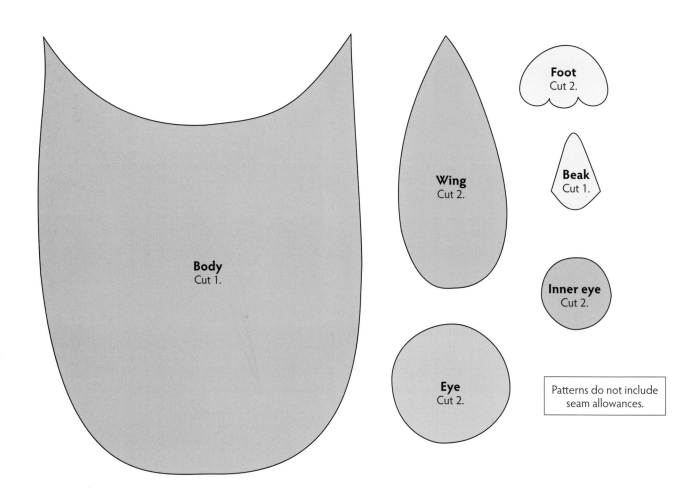

Body
Cut 1.

Wing
Cut 2.

Eye
Cut 2.

Foot
Cut 2.

Beak
Cut 1.

Inner eye
Cut 2.

Patterns do not include seam allowances.

Outside the Cabin

Here is a lap quilt with just the right amounts of scrappy and cozy. The embroidered vines add a surprising extra dimension to your quilt.

Finished size: 37½" x 51"

Block size: 7" x 7"; 13½" x 13½" with borders

Materials

Yardage is based on 42"-wide fabric unless otherwise noted.

1 yard of dark-green print for outer border and binding

⅔ yard of medium-green print for block borders

½ yard of red print for blocks and inner border

⅓ yard of black print for block borders

¼ yard *each* of tan and purple prints for blocks

⅛ yard *each* of blue, yellow, and orange prints for blocks

1⅔ yards of fabric for backing

45" x 58" piece of batting

Green pearl cotton or embroidery floss

95 buttons, ⅛" to ³⁄₁₆" diameter

Cutting

From the tan print, cut:
2 strips, 2½" x 42"; crosscut into 24 squares, 2½" x 2½"

From the red print, cut:
2 strips, 2½" x 42"; crosscut into 24 squares, 2½" x 2½"
4 strips, 2" x 42"

From the blue print, cut:
2 strips, 1¼" x 42"; crosscut into 24 rectangles, 1¼" x 2½"

From the yellow print, cut:
2 strips, 1¼" x 42"; crosscut into 24 rectangles, 1¼" x 3¼"

From the orange print, cut:
2 strips, 1¼" x 42"; crosscut into 24 rectangles, 1¼" x 3¼"

From the purple print, cut:
3 strips, 1¼" x 42"; crosscut into 24 rectangles, 1¼" x 4"

From the black print, cut:
6 strips, 1½" x 42"

From the medium-green print, cut:
7 strips, 2¾" x 42"

From the dark-green print, cut:
5 strips, 4" x 42"
5 strips, 2¼" x 42"

Assembling the Blocks

1 Draw a diagonal line from corner to corner on the wrong side of each tan square.

2 Place a marked square on a red square with right sides together. Sew a running stitch on the drawn line. At the end of the seam, take a small backstitch, but *do not* cut the thread.

3 Trim the excess fabric, leaving ¼" seam allowances. Open the fabric pieces and finger-press the seam allowances toward the red triangle.

4 Sew a running stitch a scant ¼" from the seam. Be sure the topstitching catches the seam allowances underneath. When you reach the end of the seam, knot the thread on the wrong side and cut it. Make 24 half-square-triangle units.

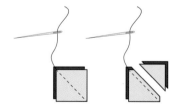

Make 24.

5 Lay a blue rectangle on one of the half-square-triangle units with right sides together, orienting the triangles as shown. Join them with Double Stitch (page 8). Finger-press the seam allowances toward the rectangle.

6 Lay a yellow rectangle on the assembled unit as shown and join them with Double Stitch. Finger-press the seam allowances toward the rectangle.

7 Add an orange rectangle in the same way, and then add a purple rectangle. Finger-press the seam allowances toward each new rectangle. Make 24 units.

Make 24.

8 Arrange four units so the half-square triangles form a pinwheel. Sew the units together in pairs, using Double Stitch and matching the intersecting seams. Finger-press the seam allowances toward the left unit in the top pair, and toward the right unit in the bottom pair.

9 Using Double Stitch, join the pairs and press the seam allowances downward, to make a block center. Make six.

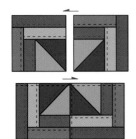 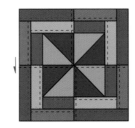

Make 6.

Adding Borders and Embroidery

Each block will be individually bordered in black and medium-green before the blocks are joined to make the quilt top.

1 Measure each block through the center from top to bottom and find the average measurement. Cut 12 pieces from the black 1½"-wide strips to this measurement (approximately 7½" long).

2 Using Double Stitch, sew the border strips to the sides of the block, finger-pressing the seam allowances toward the borders.

3 Measure the width of each block and border unit through the center and find the average measurement. Cut 12 pieces from the black 1½"-wide strips to this measurement (approximately 9½" long).

4 Use Double Stitch to sew the black border strips to the top and bottom edges of each block. Finger-press the seam allowances toward the borders.

5 Repeat steps 1–4 to cut and attach medium-green 2¾"-wide border strips to each block. The border strips will be cut approximately 9½" and 14" long.

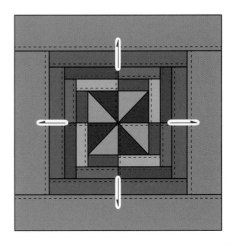

6 Transfer the embroidery design from page 47 onto the top and bottom borders of each block, referring to "Hand Embroidery" on page 12 for instructions and the photo on page 43 for placement. Embroider the vines with one strand of green pearl cotton or three strands of embroidery floss, using a backstitch for the vine and lazy daisy stitches for the leaves.

7 Arrange the bordered blocks in three rows of two, rotating alternate blocks as shown. Use Double Stitch to join the two blocks in each row, finger-pressing the seam allowances toward the longer border strips.

8 Join the rows, matching the seams, and finger-press the seam allowances downward.

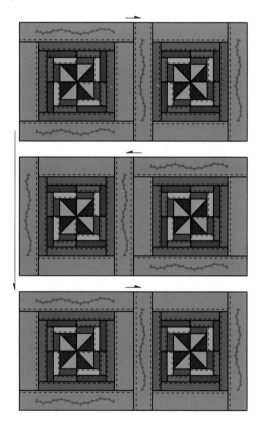

9 Repeat steps 1–4 on page 45 to cut and attach the red inner border, measuring the entire quilt top rather than a single block. The border strips will be cut approximately 41" and 30½" long. Stitch the borders onto the quilt top by hand or machine, but sew the topstitching by

hand after pressing the seam allowances toward the border.

10 Sew three of the dark-green 4"-wide strips together. Measure the quilt top through the center from top to bottom. Cut two strips the same length (approximately 44" long) from the assembled strips. Attach the strips to the sides of the quilt, pressing the seam allowances toward the outer border. Topstitch by hand. Measure the width of the quilt top, including the side borders, through the center. Cut two strips the same measurement (approximately 37½" long) from the remaining 4"-wide strips and attach them to the top and bottom edges of the quilt. Press the seam allowances toward the outer border.

Quilt assembly

11 Sew assorted small buttons along the embroidered vines, referring to the photo on page 43 for placement.

Finishing

1 Layer the backing, batting, and quilt top. Pin or baste the layers together.

2 Referring to "Quilting a Double-Stitch Project" on page 11, sew a running stitch through all layers a scant ¼" from each seam on the side without topstitching. When the quilting is complete, you will have stitching on both sides of each seamline.

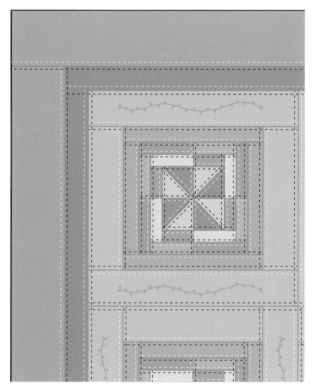

Quilting diagram

3 Trim the backing and batting even with the quilt top.

4 Join the dark-green 2¼"-wide strips to make a continuous length and use it to bind the quilt. For free, downloadable binding instructions, go to ShopMartingale.com/HowtoQuilt.

Embroidery Key

——— Backstitch

◠ Lazy daisy

Sweet Lollipops

*T*his flower-box quilt is filled with bursts of color—
flowers that are sweet as lollipops!

Finished Size: 38" x 17"

Materials

Yardage is based on 42"-wide fabric unless otherwise noted. Fat eighths measure approximately 9" x 21".

⅜ yard of dark-tan print for outer border and binding

⅓ yard of tan print for background

¼ yard of black print for inner border

1 fat eighth *each* of 3 red prints for flowers

⅛ yard of green print for stems

4" x 15" piece of green felted wool for leaves

19" x 40" piece of fusible fleece

Green pearl cotton or embroidery floss

13 buttons, ⅛" to ³⁄₁₆" diameter

Savvy Scrapping

Be adventurous and use a different red fabric for each flower. The stems can be different greens. Think of all the scraps you could use, and how diverse your garden would be!

Cutting

From the tan print, cut:
  2 strips, 1¼" x 42"; crosscut into 36 squares, 1¼" x 1¼"
  2 strips, 4" x 42"; crosscut into:
    8 squares, 4" x 4"
    5 rectangles, 4" x 7½"

From *each* of the red prints, cut:
  3 squares, 4" x 4" (9 total)

From the green print, cut:
  2 strips, 1¼" x 42"; crosscut into:
    4 rectangles, 1¼" x 4"
    5 rectangles, 1¼" x 7½"

From the black print, cut:
  3 strips, 1½" x 42"

From the dark-tan print, cut:
  2 strips, 2½" x 42"
  3 strips, 2¼" x 42"

Assembling the Table Runner

1 Draw a diagonal line from corner to corner on the wrong side of each tan 1¼" square.

2 Place a marked square on one corner of a red square with right sides together. Sew a running stitch along the drawn line to begin the Double Stitch (page 8). When you reach the end of the seam, take a small backstitch, but *do not* cut the thread.

3 Trim the excess fabric from the corner, leaving ¼" seam allowances. Open the fabric pieces and finger-press the seam allowances toward the tan triangle.

4 Bring the needle up through the seam allowances and sew a running stitch a scant ¼" from the seam. Be sure to catch the seam allowances in the topstitching. When you reach the end of the seam, knot the thread on the wrong side and cut it.

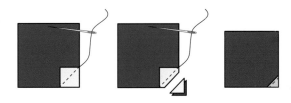

5 Repeat steps 1–4 to add a tan triangle to each corner of the red square. Make nine.

Make 9.

6 Fold a green 1¼" x 4" rectangle in half lengthwise with *wrong* sides together. Sew a running stitch ⅛" from the long raw edges. Knot and cut the thread at the end of the seam.

7 Finger-press the green fabric tube flat with the seam allowances pressed to one side and centered on the wrong side of the tube. Center this prepared stem on a tan 4" square and appliqué the stem to the square, using the method of your choice. I used an invisible slip stitch, similar to needle-turn appliqué. Make four.

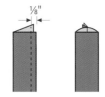

8 Repeat steps 6 and 7, using a green 1¼" x 7½" rectangle and a tan 4" x 7½" rectangle. Make five.

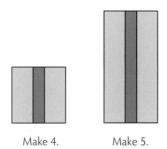

Make 4.   Make 5.

9 Arrange the flower units from step 5 in a row, creating a pleasing assortment of prints. With right sides together, use Double Stitch to join the first flower unit to a 7½"-long stem unit. Finger-press the seam allowances toward the flower unit.

10 For the second flower block, use Double Stitch to sew the flower unit to a 4"-long stem unit. Finger-press the seam allowances toward the flower unit. Sew a tan 4" square to the top of the flower unit with Double Stitch, pressing the seam allowances toward the flower unit.

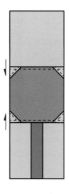

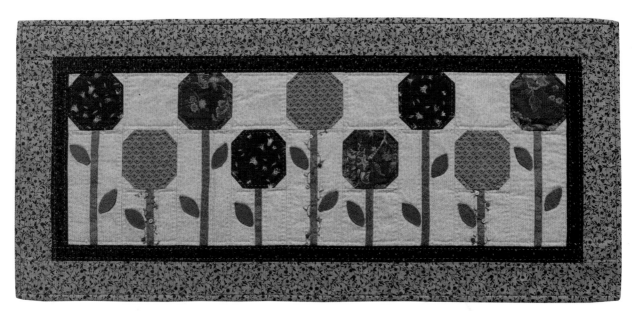

11 Repeat steps 9 and 10 to make all nine flower units, alternating long and short stems. Join the flower units with Double Stitch, matching the intersecting seams. Finger-press all the seam allowances in one direction.

Adding Borders

1 Measure the table runner through the center from top to bottom. Cut two pieces from one of the black strips to this measurement (approximately 11" long).

2 Sew an inner-border strip to each short end of the runner with Double Stitch. Press the seam allowances toward the border.

3 Measure the width of the table runner, including the newly added borders, through the center. Cut two strips from the remaining black strips to this measurement (approximately 34" long). Sew these borders to the top and bottom edges of the runner with Double Stitch, pressing the seam allowances toward the border.

4 Repeat steps 1–3 to cut and attach the dark-tan 2½"-wide outer border. The strips should measure approximately 13" and 38" long. Finger-press all seam allowances toward the outer border.

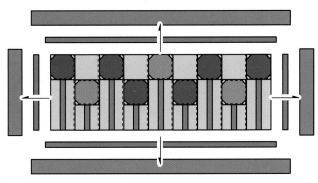

Runner assembly

Finishing

1 Transfer the embroidery designs from page 52 onto three flower blocks, referring to "Hand Embroidery" on page 12 for instructions and the photo on page 50 for placement. Trace only the vines and tiny leaves; the stems are included in the patterns for placement guidance only.

2 Measure the table runner and cut a piece of fusible fleece the same size (approximately 38" x 17"). Follow the manufacturer's instructions to fuse the fleece to the wrong side of the table runner.

3 Embroider the vines with a single strand of pearl cotton or three strands of embroidery floss, using backstitch for the vines and lazy daisy stitches for the leaves. Sew several small buttons along each vine, referring to the photo for placement.

4 Make a template from the leaf pattern on page 52 and cut 14 leaves from the green felted wool. Referring to the photo, pin the leaves to the table runner. Use pearl cotton or embroidery floss and a blanket stitch to appliqué the leaves to the table runner.

5 Layer the table-runner top and the backing fabric, wrong sides together, with the fused fleece between the fabric layers and pin or baste. Referring to "Quilting a Double-Stitch Project" on page 11, sew a running stitch through all layers a scant ¼" from each seam on the side without topstitching. When the quilting is complete, each seam will have stitching on both sides.

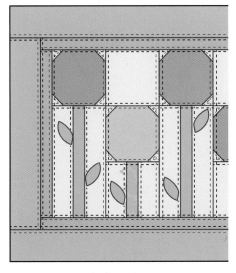

Quilting diagram

6 Trim the backing even with the table-runner top.

7 Join the dark-tan 2¼"-wide strips to make a continuous length and use it to bind the runner. For free binding instructions, go to ShopMartingale.com/HowtoQuilt.

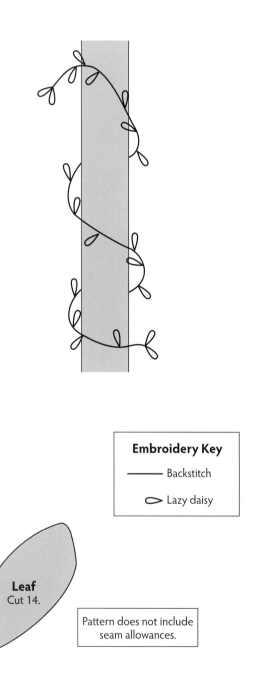

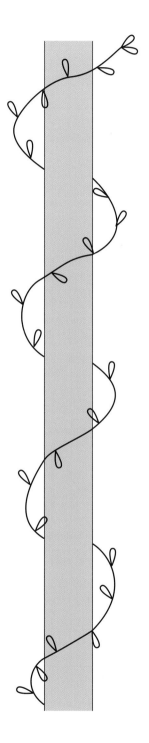

Embroidery Key

——— Backstitch

⌒ Lazy daisy

Leaf
Cut 14.

Pattern does not include seam allowances.

Winter Smiles Duo

I still love to make snowmen, whether out of snow, fabric, felt, or even Styrofoam. The smiling faces of these simple creatures warm the heart.

Winter Smiles Pillow

This easy and cheerful pillow will soon be a winter favorite. What a happy addition to any decor!

Finished Size: 14" x 14"

Materials

Yardage is based on 42"-wide fabric unless otherwise noted. Fat eighths measure approximately 9" x 21".

⅛ yard *or* 1 fat eighth *each* of 4 different blue prints for block and outer border

⅛ yard *or* 1 fat eighth of tan print for inner border

8½" x 8½" square of white print for face

Scraps of navy felted wool or solid fabric for eyes

Scrap of orange felted wool for nose

½ yard of blue print for pillow back

16" x 16" piece of fusible fleece

Pearl cotton or embroidery floss in navy blue and orange

2 light-colored triangular buttons, about ¼" wide, for eye highlights

7 assorted dark buttons, ½" to ⅝" diameter, for smile

14" x 14" pillow form

Cutting

From *each* of the blue prints, cut:
  1 strip, 2½" x 14½" (4 total)
  1 square, 2½" x 2½" (4 total)

From the tan print, cut:
  1 strip, 1¼" x 42"; crosscut into:
  2 strips, 1¼" x 8½"
  2 strips, 1¼" x 10½"

From the blue print for pillow back, cut:
  2 rectangles, 14½" x 20"*

*Before cutting, see "Finishing" on page 56.

Assembling the Pillow Front

1 Draw a diagonal line from corner to corner on the wrong side of each blue 2½" square.

2 Place a marked square on one corner of the white 8½" square, right sides together, as shown in step 4 on page 55. Sew a running stitch on the drawn line to begin the Double Stitch (page 8). At the end of the seam, take a small backstitch, but *do not* cut the thread.

3 Trim the excess fabric, leaving ¼" seam allowances. Open the fabric pieces and finger-press the seam allowances toward the blue triangle.

4 Bring the needle up through the seam allowances and sew a running stitch a scant ¼" from the seam. Be sure to catch the seam allowances underneath the topstitching. When you reach the end of the seam, knot the thread on the wrong side and cut it.

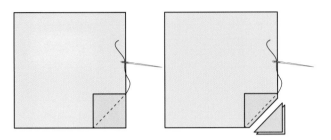

5 Repeat steps 2–4 to add a blue triangle to each corner of the white square.

6 Sew a tan 1¼" x 8½" strip to each side of the block, using Double Stitch. Finger-press the seam allowances toward the border.

7 Sew the tan 1¼" x 10½" strips to the top and bottom edges of the block, using Double Stitch. Finger-press the seam allowances toward the border.

8 Arrange the blue 2½" x 14½" strips as desired for the outer border. Trim the strips for the side borders to 2½" x 10½". Add the side borders as in step 6, and then attach the top and bottom outer-border strips.

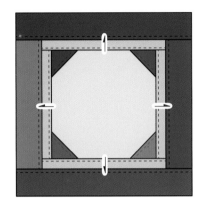

Pillow-front assembly

Quilting and Embellishing

1 Measure the pillow front and cut a piece of fusible fleece the same size (approximately 14½" x 14½"). Follow the manufacturer's instructions to fuse the fleece to the wrong side of the pillow front.

2 Referring to "Quilting a Double-Stitch Project" on page 11, sew a running stitch through all layers a scant ¼" from each seam on the side without topstitching. When the quilting is complete, you'll have stitching on both sides of each seamline.

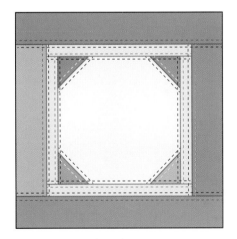

Quilting diagram

3 Using the patterns on page 60, cut two navy eyes and one orange nose from the felted wool. If you are using fabric rather than felted wool for the eyes, you may choose to add seam allowances for needle-turn appliqué or apply the embellishments with fusible web.

4 Pin the appliqués to the pillow front as shown. Stitch around the edges with a blanket stitch, using one strand of pearl cotton or three strands of embroidery floss.

5 For the smile, lightly mark seven dots on the center block. Sew a dark button at each dot. Sew a triangular button to each eye as shown, creating highlights.

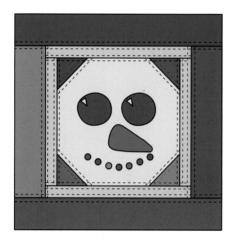

Smiles for All

Mix and match button shapes and shades, and have fun with your snowman's smile. If you prefer, small round buttons work just as well as triangular buttons for eye highlights.

Finishing

I used simple overlapping flaps for the pillow back, but you can use another method if you prefer. Begin by measuring your pillow front, which should be approximately 14½" x 14½"; if not, adjust the backing rectangles to fit.

1 Fold the two blue 14½" x 20" rectangles in half, wrong sides together, and press. The rectangles should each measure 10" x 14½" when folded.

2 Place the pillow front right side up on a flat surface and lay one folded rectangle on it, aligning the raw edges. The folded edge will lie across the pillow front as shown.

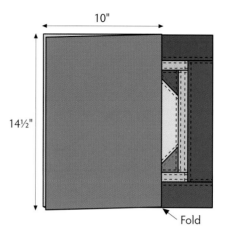

10"

14½"

Fold

3 Lay the other folded rectangle on top, aligning the raw edges on the opposite side of the pillow front. The folded edge will overlap the first pillow back. Pin the layers together along the raw edges, especially at the corners and overlapped areas. Using a ¼" seam allowance, sew around the entire pillow cover with your sewing machine.

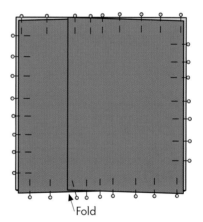

Fold

4 Turn the pillow cover right side out through the opening in the pillow back. Gently smooth the corners into shape. Insert the pillow form through the opening in the back.

Winter Smiles Wall Hanging

Happy and cheerful, times three! Bring smiling snowmen indoors to brighten up your winter home.

Finished size: 14½" x 42½"

Block size: 14" x 14"

Materials

Yardage is based on 42"-wide fabric unless otherwise noted.

¼ yard of white print for faces

¼ yard of tan print for inner borders

¼ yard *each* of 4 different dark-blue prints for blocks and outer borders

Scraps of navy felted wool for eyes

Scrap of orange felted wool for noses

1¼ yards of fabric for backing

¼ yard of navy-blue print for binding

17" x 45" piece of fusible fleece

Pearl cotton or embroidery floss in navy blue and orange

6 light-colored triangular or round buttons, about ¼" wide, for eye highlights

24 assorted dark buttons, ½" to ⅝" diameter, for smiles

Cutting

From the white print, cut:
1 strip, 8½" x 42"; crosscut into 3 squares, 8½" x 8½"

From *each* of the dark-blue prints, cut:
2 strips, 2½" x 42" (8 total)
3 squares, 2½" x 2½" (12 total)

From the tan print, cut:
4 strips, 1½" x 42"; crosscut into:
6 strips, 1½" x 8½"
6 strips, 1½" x 10½"

From the navy-blue print, cut:
4 strips, 2¼" x 42"

Assembling the Wall Hanging

1 Draw a diagonal line from corner to corner on the wrong side of each dark-blue square.

2 Place a marked square on one corner of a white square with right sides together. Sew a running stitch along the drawn line to begin the Double Stitch (page 8). At the end of the seam, take a small backstitch, but *do not* cut the thread.

3 Trim the excess fabric, leaving ¼" seam allowances. Open the fabric pieces and finger-press the seam allowances toward the dark-blue triangle.

4 Bring the needle up through the seam allowances and sew a running stitch a scant ¼" from the seam, catching the seam allowances underneath. When you reach the end of the seam, knot the thread on the wrong side and cut it.

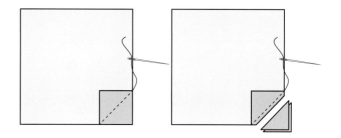

5 Repeat steps 2–4 to add a blue triangle to each corner of the white square, using a different print in each corner. Make three.

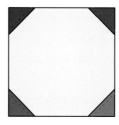

Make 3.

6 Sew a tan 1½" x 8½" strip to each side of the assembled unit, using Double Stitch. Finger-press the seam allowances toward the border.

7 Sew tan 1½" x 10½" strips to the top and bottom edges of the unit, using Double Stitch. Finger-press the seam allowances toward the border. Repeat to make three units.

8 Arrange the dark-blue 2½" x 42" strips as desired around each of the assembled units; you will use three pieces from each of the four fabrics. Trim the side borders to measure 2½" x 10½"; trim the top and bottom borders to measure 2½" x 14½".

9 Using Double Stitch, sew the side borders to each assembled unit, pressing the seam allowances toward the border. Sew the top and bottom borders to each unit in the same way.

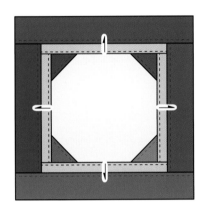

Block assembly

10 Arrange the three assembled blocks in a vertical column. Join the blocks with Double Stitch, pressing the seam allowances downward.

Appliquéing and Embellishing

1 Measure the wall hanging and cut a piece of fusible fleece the same size (approximately 14½" x 42½"). Follow the manufacturer's instructions to fuse the fleece to the wrong side of the wall hanging.

2 Using the patterns on page 60, cut six navy eyes and three orange noses from the wool.

3 Pin the eyes and noses to the blocks and use your favorite appliqué method to stitch them to the wall hanging. I used a blanket stitch, and one strand of matching pearl cotton.

4 Lightly mark eight button locations for each snowman's smile. Sew one of the ½"- to ⅝"-diameter dark buttons at each location. Sew a triangular or round button to each eye as shown, creating a highlight.

Wall-hanging assembly

Finishing

1 Cut the backing fabric in half to create two 22" lengths. Remove the selvages and sew the pieces together along one short edge. Trim the pieced backing approximately 3" larger than the wall-hanging top on all sides. Layer the quilt backing and wall-hanging top, wrong sides together, with the fused fleece between the fabric layers. Pin or baste the layers together.

2 Referring to "Quilting a Double-Stitch Project" on page 11, sew a running stitch through all layers a scant ¼" from each seam on the side without topstitching. When the quilting is complete, each seam will have stitching on both sides.

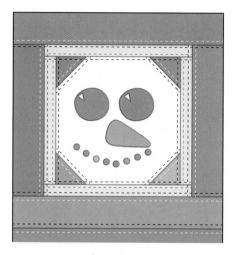

Quilting diagram

3 Trim the edges of the backing even with the wall-hanging top.

4 Join the navy 2¼"-wide strips to make a continuous length; use it to bind the wall hanging. For free binding instructions, go to ShopMartingale.com/HowtoQuilt.

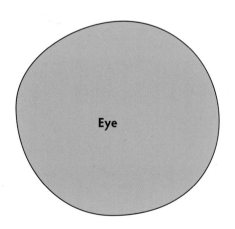

Eye

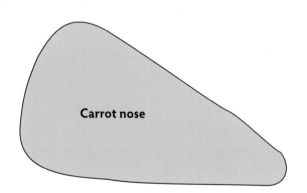

Carrot nose

String Happy

This project uses what we will call "strings," the uneven ends cut from fabric yardage. And doesn't using scraps make all quilters happy?

Finished Size: 30½" x 30½"

Materials

Yardage is based on 42"-wide fabric unless otherwise noted.

1 yard of muslin for foundations

Lots of assorted strings, strips, and scraps (approximately 1 yard total) for blocks

⅝ yard of black print for blocks and binding

1 yard of fabric for backing

36" x 36" piece of batting

Stringing Along

After you wash and dry a piece of fabric, you have an uneven, ratty edge to trim and square up. Rather than trimming just ¼" or so, cut a couple of inches from the edge and toss it into a basket. Your collection of strings will grow, and you can use them in this project. If you don't have a supply of strings yet, use strips of various widths cut from your fabric stash. Any strip at least ¾" wide and 6½" long will work for this project.

Cutting

From the muslin, cut:
5 strips, 6½" x 42"; crosscut into 25 squares, 6½" x 6½"

From the black print, cut:
5 strips, 2" x 42"; crosscut into 100 squares, 2" x 2"
4 strips, 2¼" x 42"

Assembling the Blocks

1 Place a fabric string along the top edge of a muslin square, right sides up. Rather than aligning the sides and top, allow the string to extend past the muslin edges.

2 Place a second string on top of the first, right sides together, aligning only the lower edges. The edges may be straight or at an angle—either way is fine.

3 Using a ¼" seam allowance, sew a running stitch along the matched edges through both strings and the muslin foundation. At the end of the *foundation*, take a backstitch, but *do not* cut the thread.

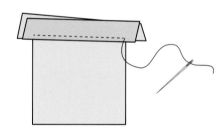

4 Open the fabric strings, fold the second string down onto the foundation, and finger-press the seam allowances toward the second string. Bring the threaded needle up through all layers and sew a running stitch along the top of the second string a scant ¼" from the seam. Be sure to catch the foundation and seam allowances in this topstitching. At the far edge of the foundation, knot the thread on the wrong side and cut it. It's not necessary to trim the strings as

you work; just let them extend beyond the sides of the muslin until the string piecing is complete.

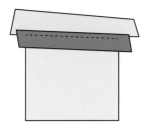

5 Place a new string on the lower edge of the second string, right sides together, aligning the lower edges. Attach the new string with Double Stitch (page 8). Continue adding strings in this way until the entire muslin foundation is covered.

6 When the foundation is completely covered with fabric strings, flip the entire block over on a cutting mat and trim the strings even with the muslin foundation, creating a 6½" x 6½" block. Make 25.

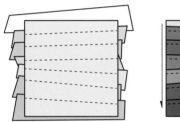
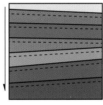

7 Draw a diagonal line from corner to corner on the wrong side of each black 2" square.

8 Place a marked square on one corner of a string-pieced block, right sides together, aligning the raw edges as shown in step 9. Sew a running stitch along the drawn line. At the end of the seam, take a small backstitch, but *do not* cut the thread.

9 Trim the excess fabric, leaving ¼" seam allowances. Open the fabric pieces and finger-press toward the black triangle. Bring the threaded needle up through the seam allowances and sew a running stitch a scant ¼" from the seam.

Be sure to catch the seam allowances with the topstitching. When you reach the end of the seam, knot the thread on the wrong side and cut it.

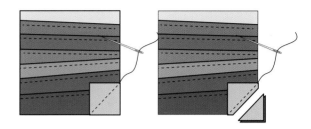

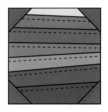

10 Repeat steps 8 and 9 to add a black triangle to each corner of the block. Make 25 blocks.

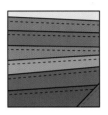

Assembling the Quilt Top

1 Arrange the finished blocks in five rows of five blocks each, alternating the direction of the strings to add interest.

2 Join the blocks in the top row with Double Stitch. Finger-press the seam allowances toward the right.

Strong Stitches

For a stronger quilt, you may choose to sew the first part of the Double Stitch by machine when assembling the quilt top. Always sew the topstitching by hand with a running stitch to preserve the Double-Stitch appearance in the finished quilt.

---

3 In the same way, assemble the blocks in the second row, but finger-press the seam allowances toward the left. Assemble the remaining three rows, alternating the pressing direction from row to row.

4 To join the rows, match the intersecting seams and nestle the seam allowances, holding the pieces in place with pins. Join the pieces, using Double Stitch and finger-pressing the seam allowances downward.

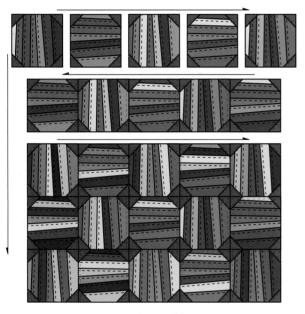

Quilt assembly

Finishing

1 Layer the backing, batting, and quilt top. Pin or baste the layers together.

2 Referring to "Quilting a Double-Stitch Project" on page 11, sew a running stitch through all layers a scant ¼" from each seam on the side without topstitching. When the quilting is complete, each seam will have stitching on both sides.

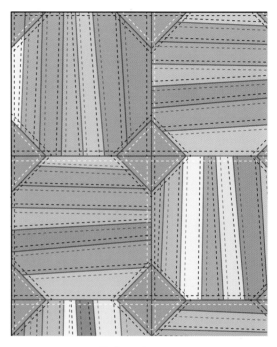

Quilting diagram

3 Trim the batting and backing even with the quilt top.

4 Join the black 2¼"-wide strips to make a continuous length and use it to bind the quilt. For free, downloadable binding instructions, go to ShopMartingale.com/HowtoQuilt.

Looks Like Spring

A pair of easily pieced flowers, complete with leaves and stems, welcome the season or help you bring it indoors any time of year.

Finished Size: 22½" x 23½"

Materials

Yardage is based on 42"-wide fabric unless otherwise noted.

½ yard of tan print for background

⅛ yard *each* of red, burgundy, and pink prints for flowers

¼ yard of blue print for outer border

¼ yard of dark-blue print #2 for binding

¼ yard of green print for stems and leaves

⅛ yard of dark-blue print #1 for inner border

¾ yard of fabric for backing

25" x 26" piece of fusible fleece

Black pearl cotton or embroidery floss

2 bug-shaped buttons, approximately ¾" x 1"

Cutting

From the tan print, cut:
  2 strips, 4¼" x 42"; crosscut into:
    2 rectangles, 4¼" x 7½" (A and E)
    2 rectangles, 4¼" x 2½" (B and G)
    1 rectangle, 4¼" x 3½" (C)
    1 rectangle, 4¼" x 4½" (F)
    1 rectangle, 4¼" x 6½" (D)
    1 rectangle, 4¼" x 9½" (H)
  2 strips, 2½" x 42"; crosscut into:
    20 squares, 2½" x 2½"
    1 rectangle, 2½" x 8½"

From the red print, cut:
  1 strip, 2½" x 20"; crosscut into 8 squares, 2½" x 2½"

From the burgundy print, cut:
  1 strip, 2½" x 20"; crosscut into 8 squares, 2½" x 2½"

From the pink print, cut:
  1 strip, 2½" x 20"; crosscut into 4 squares, 2½" x 2½"

From the green print, cut:
  4 squares, 2½" x 2½"
  1 rectangle, 1" x 9½"
  1 rectangle, 1" x 11½"

From dark-blue print #1, cut:
  2 strips, 1½" x 42"

From the blue print, cut:
  3 strips, 2½" x 42"

From dark-blue print #2, cut:
  3 strips, 2¼" x 42"

Piecing the Flowers

1 Draw a diagonal line from corner to corner on the wrong side of 12 tan squares and all four pink squares.

2 Place a marked tan square on a red square with right sides together. Sew a running stitch along the drawn line. When you reach the end of the seam, take a small backstitch, but *do not* cut the thread.

3 Trim the excess fabric, leaving ¼" seam allowances. Open the fabric pieces and finger-press the seam allowances toward the red triangle.

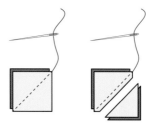

4 Bring the needle up through the seam allowances and sew a running stitch a scant ¼" from the seam. Be sure to catch the seam allowances with this topstitching. At the end of the seam, knot the thread on the wrong side and cut it. Make six tan/red units, six tan/burgundy units, two pink/red units, and two pink/burgundy units. Finger-press the seam allowances toward the darker fabric in each half-square-triangle unit.

5 Arrange the half-square-triangle units to make two flower blocks, one primarily red and one mostly burgundy. Each block is made from four tan squares and eight half-square-triangle units, arranged in three rows of four square units each.

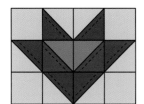
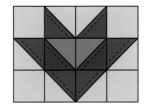

6 Assemble each flower-block row with Double Stitch (page 8). Finger-press the seam allowances to one side as shown.

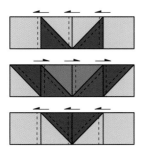

7 Join the rows of each flower block with Double Stitch. Press the seam allowances upward in the burgundy flower block, which will be on the left in the quilt. Press the seam allowances downward in the red flower block. Match the seam intersections, pinning before you stitch.

8 Sew the tan 2½" x 8½" rectangle to the top of the burgundy flower block with Double Stitch. Finger-press the seam allowances toward the tan rectangle.

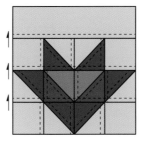
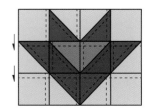

Piecing the Stems and Leaves

1 Draw a diagonal line from corner to corner on the wrong side of each green square. Place a marked square on the lower-right corner of rectangle A with right sides together. Sew a running stitch along the drawn line. At the end of the seam, take a small backstitch, but *do not* cut the thread.

2 Trim the excess fabric, leaving ¼" seam allowances. Bring the threaded needle up through the seam allowances and sew a running stitch a scant ¼" from the seam. Be sure to catch the seam allowances with this topstitching. When you reach the end of the seam, knot the thread on the wrong side and cut it.

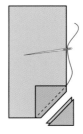

3 Repeat steps 1 and 2 to add green corner triangles to the lower-left corner of rectangle C, the upper-right corner of rectangle F, and the upper-left corner of rectangle H.

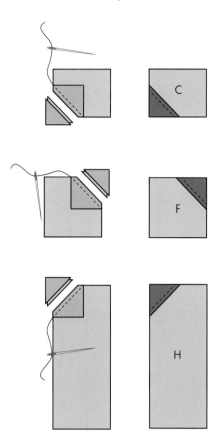

4 Arrange the background and green stem rectangles in two units as shown above right. Join rectangles A and B; C and D; E and F; and G and H with Double Stitch, finger-pressing the seam allowances as shown.

5 Stitch the assembled background sections to the stem rectangles with Double Stitch. Finger-press the seam allowances toward the green rectangles.

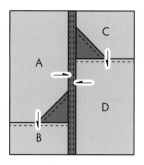

Left stem unit

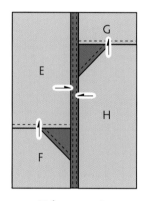

Right stem unit

6 Sew the burgundy flower unit to the left stem unit with Double Stitch. Finger-press the seam allowances toward the flower unit. Double Stitch the red flower unit to the right stem unit. Finger-press the seam allowances toward the stem unit.

7 Place the completed side sections right sides together, matching the intersecting seams, which should nestle neatly. Pin and use Double Stitch to join the sections. Finger-press the seam allowances toward the right side.

Adding Borders

1 Measure the quilt top through the center from top to bottom. Cut two pieces from the 1½"-wide dark-blue #1 strips to this measurement (approximately 17½" long).

2 Sew a border strip to each side of the quilt with Double Stitch. Press the seam allowances toward the border.

3 Measure the width of the quilt top, including the side borders, through the center from side to side. Cut two pieces from the 1½"-wide dark-blue #1 strips to this measurement (approximately 18½" long).

4 Use Double Stitch to sew the border strips to the top and bottom edges of the quilt. Finger-press the seam allowances toward the border.

5 Repeat steps 1–4 to cut and attach the blue 2½"-wide outer border. The border strips will be cut approximately 19½" and 22½" long. Finger-press all seam allowances toward the outer border.

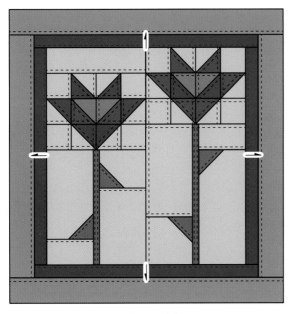

Quilt assembly

Finishing

1 Transfer the embroidery design from page 70 onto the quilt, referring to "Hand Embroidery" on page 12 for instructions and the photo on page 65 for placement.

2 Measure the quilt top and cut a piece of fusible fleece the same size (approximately 22½" x 23½"). Follow the manufacturer's instructions to fuse the fleece to the wrong side of the quilt.

Fabulous Fusible

Fusible fleece is an easy-to-quilt lightweight batting that also works as a great stabilizer for the embroidery and buttons.

3 Embroider the design using a running stitch and black pearl cotton or embroidery floss. Sew a bug-shaped button at the top end of each line of stitching.

4 Layer the quilt top and backing with wrong sides together, with the fused fleece between the fabric layers. Pin or baste the layers together. Referring to "Quilting a Double-Stitch Project" on page 11, sew a running stitch through all layers a scant ¼" from each seam on the side without topstitching. When the quilting is complete, each seam will have stitching on both sides.

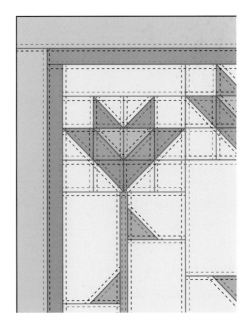

Quilting diagram

5 Join the 2¼"-wide dark-blue #2 strips to make a continuous length and use it to bind the quilt. For free, downloadable binding instructions, go to ShopMartingale.com/HowtoQuilt.

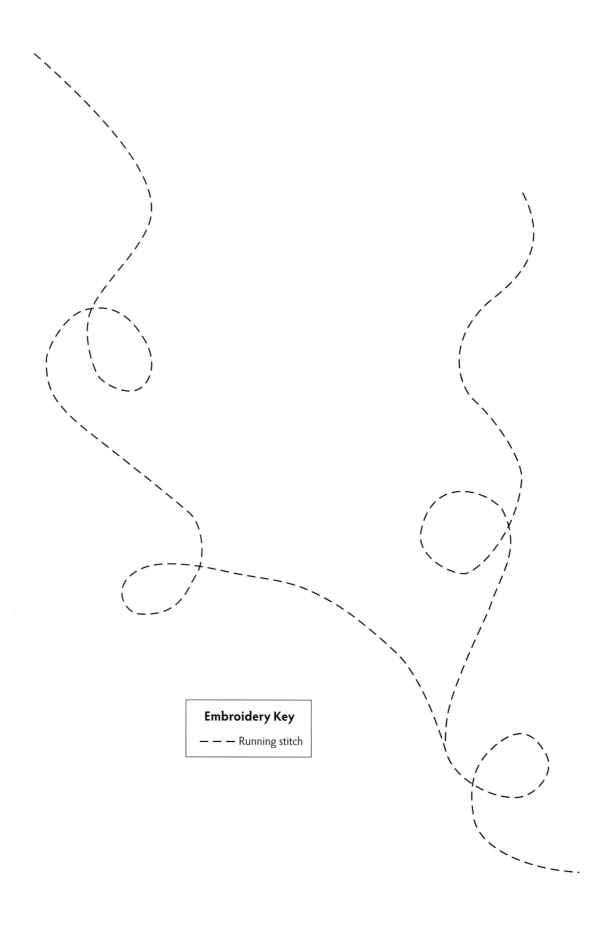

Embroidery Key

– – – Running stitch

We Are United

*T*here's never a time of year when the patriotic combination of red, white, and blue isn't in season.

Designed by Kathleen Brown; made by Anne Styles
Finished Size: 36" x 20"

Materials

Yardage is based on 42"-wide fabric unless otherwise noted.

½ yard of tan print for outer border

½ yard *total* of assorted off-white prints for blocks and star background

⅓ yard *total* of assorted red prints for blocks

⅛ yard of dark-blue print for inner border

Scraps of assorted dark-blue fabrics for stars

¼ yard of multicolored print for binding

¾ yard of fabric for backing

38" x 22" piece of fusible fleece

Off-white pearl cotton or embroidery floss

Stash Busting

Use your stash and put many different red and off-white prints into your table runner.

Cutting

From the assorted off-white prints, cut a *total* of:
50 squares, 2½" x 2½"
1 rectangle, 6½" x 10½"

From the assorted red prints, cut a *total* of:
50 squares, 2½" x 2½"

From the dark-blue print, cut:
2 strips, 1½" x 42"

From the tan print, cut:
3 strips, 4½" x 42"

From the multicolored print, cut:
3 strips, 2¼" x 42"

Assembling the Table Runner

1 Draw a diagonal line from corner to corner on the wrong side of each off-white 2½" square.

2 Place a marked square on a red square, right sides together. Sew a running stitch on the drawn line. When you reach the end of the seam, take a small backstitch, but *do not* cut the thread.

3 Trim the excess fabric, leaving ¼" seam allowances. Open the fabric pieces and finger-press the seam allowances toward the red triangle.

4 Bring the needle to the right side of the red fabric through the seam allowances and sew a running stitch a scant ¼" from the seam. Be sure this line of topstitching catches the seam allowances underneath. At the end of the seam, knot the thread on the wrong side and cut it. Make 50 half-square-triangle units.

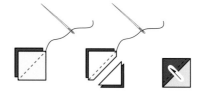

5 Arrange the 50 half-square-triangle units in five rows of 10 units each, with the red triangles in the lower-right corner of each unit. Join the units in each row, using Double Stitch (page 8). Press the seam allowances toward the

left in rows 1, 3, and 5 and toward the right in rows 2 and 4.

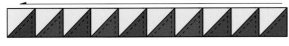

Rows 1, 3, and 5

Rows 2 and 4

6 Join the rows with Double Stitch. Press the seam allowances downward.

7 Sew the off-white 6½" x 10½" rectangle to the left edge of the assembled rows, using Double Stitch. Press the seam allowances toward the rectangle.

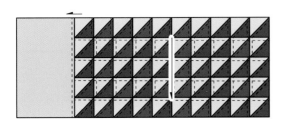

Adding Borders

1 Measure the table runner through the center from top to bottom. Cut two pieces from the dark-blue 1½"-wide strips to this measurement (approximately 10½" long). For efficient fabric use, cut one side border from each of the two dark-blue strips.

2 Sew a border strip to each short end of the table runner with Double Stitch. Finger-press the seam allowances toward the border.

3 Measure the width of the table runner, including the side borders, through the center from side to side. Cut two pieces from the dark-blue 1½"-wide strips to this measurement (approximately 28½" long). Sew these border strips to the top and bottom edges of the table runner as directed in step 2.

4 Repeat steps 1–3 to measure, cut, and attach the tan 4½"-wide outer border. The border strips will be cut approximately 12½" and 36½" long. Finger-press the seam allowances toward the outer border.

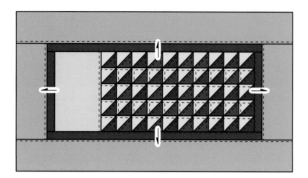

Quilt assembly

Finishing

1 Measure the table runner and cut a piece of fusible fleece the same size (approximately 36" x 20"). Follow the manufacturer's instructions to fuse the fleece to the wrong side of the table runner.

2 Using the pattern below right, prepare five stars for your favorite appliqué method, using the scraps of assorted dark-blue fabrics. The sample uses raw-edge appliqué. The stars were cut without seam allowance, pinned to the quilt, and sewn in place with a running stitch ⅛" from the stars' raw edges. Use one strand of off-white pearl cotton or three strands of embroidery floss to attach the appliqués.

3 Layer the backing and table runner, wrong sides together, with the fused fleece between the fabric layers. Pin or baste the layers together.

4 Referring to "Quilting a Double-Stitch Project" on page 11, sew a running stitch through all layers a scant ¼" from each seam on the side without topstitching. When the quilting is complete, you'll have stitching on both sides of each seamline.

Quilting diagram

5 Trim the backing even with the table-runner top.

6 Join the multicolored 2¼"-wide strips to make a continuous length and use it to bind the runner. For free binding instructions, go to ShopMartingale.com/HowtoQuilt.

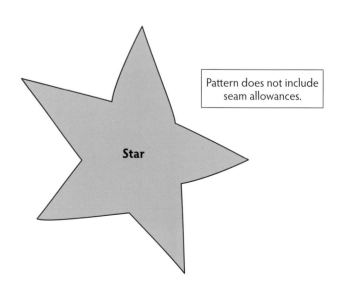

Pattern does not include seam allowances.

Star

Partly Cloudy

When the sky changes from blue to dark purple, and then the sun shines through the clouds, the colors are spectacular. Capture those colors in this little quilt, and imagine a soft breeze that parts the clouds so the sun shines through.

Finished size: 14½" x 14½"

Block size: 9" x 9"

Materials

Yardage is based on 42"-wide fabric unless otherwise noted. Fat eighths measure approximately 9" x 21".

1 fat eighth *each* of light-blue, dark-blue, light-purple, dark-purple, and dark-yellow prints for block

¼ yard of yellow print for outer border

⅛ yard of dark-gray print for inner border

17" x 17" piece of fusible fleece

Green pearl cotton or embroidery floss

15 buttons, ⅛" to ¼" diameter

Cutting

From the light-purple print, cut:
  3 squares, 3½" x 3½"; cut the squares into quarters diagonally to yield 12 triangles

From the dark-purple print, cut:
  1 square, 3½" x 3½"; cut the square into quarters diagonally to yield 4 triangles

From the dark-yellow print, cut:
  4 squares, 3½" x 3½"; cut the squares into quarters diagonally to yield 16 triangles

From *each* of the dark-blue and light-blue prints, cut:
  4 squares, 3⅛" x 3⅛"; cut each square in half diagonally to yield 2 triangles (8 of each color; 16 total)

From the dark-gray print, cut:
  1 strip, 1¼" x 42"

From the yellow print, cut:
  2 strips, 2¼" x 42"

Assembling the Block

1 Place a light-purple triangle and a dark-yellow triangle with right sides together. Join the triangles, using Double Stitch (page 8). Sew a running stitch seam and take a small backstitch at the end, but *do not* cut the thread. Be careful not to stretch the bias seams.

2 Open the fabric pieces and finger-press the seam allowances toward the purple triangle. Come up through the seam allowances and sew a running stitch a scant ¼" from the seam. Be sure the topstitching also catches the seam allowances underneath. At the end of the seam, knot the thread on the wrong side and cut it. Make 12 light-purple/dark-yellow units and four dark-purple/dark-yellow units.

Make 12.   Make 4.

3 Sew a light-blue triangle to a light-purple/dark-yellow unit as shown, using Double Stitch. Make eight light-purple/dark-yellow/light-blue units, four light-purple/dark-yellow/dark-blue units, and four dark-purple/dark-yellow/dark-blue units.

Make 8.   Make 4.   Make 4.

4 Arrange the units in four rows of four units each. Orient the units as shown so that the center units form a pinwheel. Using Double Stitch, join the units into rows. Finger-press the seam allowances in alternating directions for each row.

5 Join the rows together with Double Stitch. Match the intersecting seams, nesting the seam allowances, and pin if you wish before stitching. Finger-press the seam allowances downward.

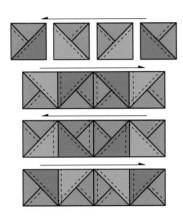

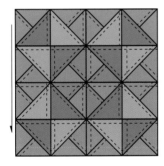

Adding Borders

1 Measure the block through the center from top to bottom. Cut two pieces from the dark-gray 1¼"-wide strip to this measurement (approximately 9½" long).

2 Using Double Stitch, sew a border strip to each side of the block, finger-pressing the seam allowances toward the border.

3 Measure the width of the block and border strips through the center. Cut two pieces from the dark-gray 1¼"-wide strip to this measurement (approximately 11" long).

4 Use Double Stitch to sew the border strips to the top and bottom edges of the block, pressing the seam allowances toward the border.

5 Repeat steps 1–4 to cut and attach the yellow 2¼"-wide outer border. The border strips will be cut approximately 11" and 14½" long. Finger-press all seam allowances toward the outer border.

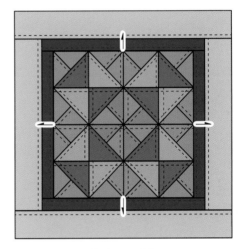

Quilt assembly

Finishing

1 Transfer the embroidery design from page 78 onto the quilt, referring to "Hand Embroidery" on page 12 for instructions and the photo on page 75 for placement. Extend the design as necessary to fit on the longer bottom border.

2 Measure the quilt top and cut a piece of fusible fleece the same size (approximately 14½" x 14½"). Follow the manufacturer's instructions to fuse the fleece to the wrong side of the quilt.

3 Referring to "Quilting a Double-Stitch Project" on page 11, sew a running stitch through all layers a scant ¼" from each seam on the side without topstitching. When the quilting is complete, you'll have stitching on both sides of each seamline.

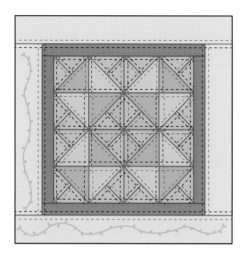

Quilting diagram

4 Embroider the vines with a backstitch and the leaves with a lazy daisy stitch, using one strand of pearl cotton or three strands of embroidery floss. Sew the small buttons along the vines, referring to the photo for placement.

5 Follow the instructions in "Framing" on page 13 to frame the finished quilt.

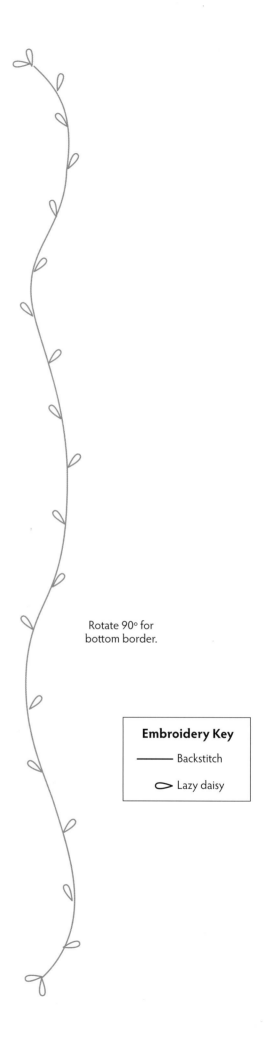

Rotate 90° for bottom border.

Embroidery Key	
———	Backstitch
⌒	Lazy daisy

Acknowledgments

I would like to take this small space to give a big thank-you to my husband, friends, and family, who have had patience with me and my deadlines and continued to love the scattered person I became while writing this book. My husband's overwhelming support and encouragement is always unending. The household chores, mostly the dusting, have taken a backseat to everything else this year, including the garden, which we affectionately call "nature at work."

I thank my dear friends DeLoyce and Sharon for their continued faith and love. A kind and sincere thank-you goes to Anne Styles for loving all things handwork. She volunteered to sew half-square triangles, and then started sewing them together. I so appreciate her enthusiasm.

A special thank-you for the team at Martingale who took the time to explain, edit, and help so much in this process. They are an understanding and experienced group to work with.

I am a great collector of fabrics and I would like to thank all of the fabric designers and manufacturers who bring us wonderful colors and textures of fabric to play and create with every day. A single pattern can be given a thousand different looks with changes in color, hue, and texture from our fabrics.

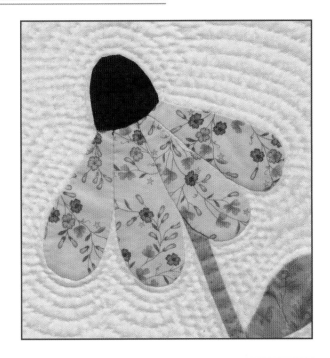

About the Author

Kathleen has been sewing for many years and quilting since 1980. In that time, she's lived and traveled all across the United States.

She became a pattern designer in 2003 and began designing for her cherished business, Mountain Patchwork. While she loves all kinds of quilting, Kathleen is especially passionate about taking some sewing along at all times, having found that a few idle minutes here and there can really make a difference in completing a project. She loves designing patterns that can be constructed with Double Stitch.

Kathleen and her husband love to camp, travel, and go on Sunday drives in the mountains. Living in western Montana gives them endless mountain roads to travel and explore, and, when they're extremely lucky, they find a new huckleberry patch! She is the grandmother of two wonderful kids, and found nothing more thrilling than the day her granddaughter asked, "Will you teach me to sew?" The answer was, "Of course!"